God, who in Thy transcendent providence wast pleased to cause thy servant, **Eugenio Pacelli,** to be numbered among the supreme pontiffs, we pray Thee to admit him, who on earth was vicar of Thy only-begotten Son, into the company of Thy holy pontiffs now and for evermore: through the same our Lord Jesus Christ, Thy Son, who is God and liveth and reigneth with Thee in the unity of the Holy Ghost, world without end.

Joe Kotcka   Amen.

A short history of IRELAND

A short history of
IRELAND

BY ROGER CHAUVIRÉ

Professor, National University of Ireland
Translated by The Earl of Wicklow

THE DEVIN-ADAIR COMPANY   1956   NEW YORK

Contents

Preface

*Lord Wicklow gently urges me to add a few lines, as a
preface, to this, his version of my little book. What am
I going to say? Someone whose name I now forget once
hinted that "a book is a confession." What? Even such
a book, supposedly "scientific"? Well, who knows? I
remember, when I was asked by the French publisher
would I be prepared to compile a short History of Ireland, I suddenly felt so full of my subject and so en-
thused that I sat down at my table and wrote the whole
thing in a month. I was working in that half dream I
know so well, which is the enchantment of memory. Why
so?*

*Ireland chances to be a small nation. That she
dearly paid for it, granted. But any drawback has its
compensation. She makes up for it in so far as she may
be grasped and, so to say, felt, with one's very senses.
She is not a distant, somewhat abstract goddess like
those huge entities, America, Germany, France; she is
a familiar acquaintance like Scotland or Venice, or those
ancient lands, Brittany, Provence, Auvergne, which
finally flocked under the fleurs-de-lis but whose hearts,
if only you cock your ear, can still be heard beating dis-
tinctly. Lorraine is far from Béarn, literally and meta-
phorically, Roussillon from Flanders; it is difficult to*

*be equally acquainted with, and fond of, them; it is not
so to keep Dungannon and Glenbeigh, Donaghadee and
Inishtiogue, in a warm corner of one's heart. When from
over here I "think long" of Ireland, Dublin I seldom
secretly recall: too prosperous, too international, too
nondifferent, too Americanized, too overladen with glittering cinemas and shining cars and fat jobs; I'd rather
recollect some lonely spot, magically surged in me, complete and visible, with its colors and lines, the whisper
of its leaves or the roar of its surf, the very fragrance of
its hay or turf or kelp.*

*More than once, the vision awakes I don't know which
stir, a sort of vague and pleasant sadness, as though that
meditative scenery, conjured up from the depths of
memory, had, too, a memory of its own, some conscious-
ness of a long and sorrowful past. And so it may have.
Ireland's history has been, indeed, full of woes and de-
feats and forlorn hopes and tears; but when the past has
become past for good, and been given the absolution
of death, something indescribably soothing oozes out of
it, as though, ordeal and bitterness being forgotten, it
only left in us the greatness of misfortune manfully
borne by those who found the gods against them. What
appeals to us most is failure, if noble. Which do you
prefer, the Risorgimento's glamour or Michelangelo's
dirge, lamenting at one sigh Florence's freedom lost and
Vittoria Colonna's parting? Which is more moving for
the imagination of man: Napoleon's trampling all over
Europe or Saint Joan's stake and Louis XVI's scaffold?
It has often occurred to me that among the nations of
the modern world, Ireland and France, twin sisters, have
had a most pathetic and, therefore, poetic history.*

*In France's case, however, whatever storms she may
have been battered by, she at least always survived as a*

*person and still is fighting for survival. Not so with Ire-
land. A Sleeping Beauty whom Death has touched with
her cold finger will awake never more. Gaelic Ireland
is gone—a lore of tradition and legend and wisdom (in
a word, of poetry again), whose loss we never will recover nor repair. Heaven forbid that I should slight the
country's latest efforts towards independence: too late,
alas, too late! It may be the independence of a state,
it cannot be the independence of a social and mental
structure which is no more. And perhaps it was bound
to be so. Gaeldom was poorly equipped to stand up to
the onslaught of outside forces, Danes, Normans, English; it was not so much a political or military system as
a network of conceptions about family and society, a
mode of thought and feeling, a way of life and, of course,
being weak for resisting assault, it had tremendous
strength for enduring, and struggling, and, after a long
agony, leaving long and bitter regrets. Look now around
us at this awful industrialized world whose flow has already half engulfed us; the rise of monstrous empires,
the ever-stretching tentacles of an ever-intruding state,
while, above all, machines of every description, cinema,
radio, daily press, television, are busy ironing out, de-
vitalizing, dehumanizing us, steadily reducing man from
a free agent to a matriculation number; from this anony-
mous, gray drabness, our mind turns with still more
poignancy to those homely and various and original ex-
pressions of man which went down in the past, Aquitaine
of the troubadours, Ireland of the Gaels, Provence of
the Félibres—civilizations that were humble, granted,
but true ones, and whose warm raciness we still dimly
guess, and in which man must have felt at ease, because
he was allowed to remain himself, because they sprang
from his very soul.*

*Sometimes I wonder and ponder. . . . Maybe, who
knows? Although reduced to a whisper, the voice of
Gaeldom is not altogether silenced, as would appear at
first glance. . . . Maybe the* genius loci *vaguely survives
in the silent regions of its people's souls. "Nous vivons
du parfum d'un vase vide," Renan once wrote in a lovely
sentence: is not that elusive fragrance the very charm
of Ireland, a charm we delight in the more that we're
never certain it won't vanish? I know, I know, there is
O'Connell Street, the hustle and bustle of the modern
world; no matter, Ireland's pulse is slow, life is still quiet
and leisurely, one is still given time to enjoy it. Look at
the age and number of the old people in the old country:
they lived long because the pace of life was slow, the
ancient and pleasant rhythm of unadulterated man. Even
among the people of the cities, an instinct lurks like a
memory of the species, an instinct dating back, no doubt,
to remote pastoral times, when work and pastimes were
regulated by the quiet circle of the seasons; their gait has
the carefree easygoingness of the shepherd's; the mind
keeps that facile yielding to the great things of life and
death, which the daily contact with the immutable laws
of nature breeds or infuses in the tranquil and sensible
peasant. More prone to take things for granted than to
ask questions, for them life is what it is, faith is faith,
as handed over by innumerable ancestors, "faith of our
fathers.". . . "We trye to live," (a letter just received
yesterday reads) "and rear our children in the Catholic
Irish traditional way." Traditional . . . That instinc-
tive mistrust of novelties—what prudence! what wisdom!
Here in Paris, the whole place is a boiling caldron: an
exhibition is hardly out than another and more won-
drous one is in; after the astounding treasures of Berlin,
the matchless mosaics of Ravenna; heaps of books,*

pictures, works of art, theories, controversies, a new philosophy of life every other morning; a permanent eruption of unquenchable curiosities; five people, five opinions. Of course, such an atmosphere is bubbling with interest and excitement; but at the end, what's the use? We know so little, we live so short a span! Beside that humming beehive, distant Ireland rises as a cloister of repose and restfulness. The fact involves, no doubt, some indulgence in mental stagnation. Well, what about it? One cannot have it both ways. If the Irish scholar was right who compared Ireland to the lotos eaters' island—when everything is said and done, lucky lotos eaters! Are they not to be envied? Can you imagine a better fortune for a human being than to have been born somewhere in County Clare, Ennistymon or Gort, and there to spend his life without asking answerless questions, and to rest among the immemorial graves in the ruined church of Liscannor, to be lulled to eternal sleep by the familiar waves?

Such is, at least for me, the unique color, such is the charm of Ireland. Have I been able, in this little epitome of her history, to convey to the casual reader—that ignorant wanderer—my feeling that there, by the ditch of his road, lies a hidden spring where poetry redundantly wells up? At least I can honestly state that my work was an earnest effort towards truth. That it also was a work of love, why should I be ashamed of confessing? Many a scholar, of a higher stature, has also fallen a prey to the same fascinating lure: to quote only two, I ask leave to inscribe here the honored names of Edmund Curtis and J. H. Delargy.

ROGER CHAUVIRÉ

Paris, France

A short history of IRELAND

I. THE
GAELIC
AGE

Chapter 1. The Land

The destiny of this people, as so often happens, is already
written in the soil. Its physical geography foretells its human geography and its history.

Ireland, on the extreme west of Europe, is a remainder
of that Northern Atlantis which, hundreds of centuries
ago, was the last protrusion of the continent into the
Ocean, and which, when its threshold had gradually sub-
sided, was divided up into lands from then onwards sepa-
rated from each other by shallow channels, the chief of
these being what are known as the British Isles. Our island itself, which is in shape more or less a rectangle with
blunted corners, bears everywhere the marks left by a
long glacial period: erratic boulders, mountain peaks
rounded off by the slow friction of the canopy of ice
which used to cover them. These mountains (the highest
of which do not reach much more than three thousand
feet) are laid out more or less in a circle, or polygon, on
the circumference of the island, while in the center there
spreads with few interruptions a wide plain, so that the

1

whole island would remind one of the form of a dish. This
has certain results: first, the almost oppressive majesty of
those landscapes on the verge of the ocean, in which the
mountains, while not especially high in themselves, appear to be of an amazing size owing to the fact that they
are on the edge of the sea and fall straight down into it;
next, there is the course of the waters, which, owing to
the fact that there is no slope, seem forever held up in
the central plain and lazily seek for an outlet, meander-
ing along, as does the Shannon, through sleepy lakes and
from marsh to marsh, till it finally escapes at the rapids of
Castleconnell. These marshes are peat bogs, a vast deposit
and a vast witness to the primeval forest which has not
yet had time to turn into coal, and has remained in the
intermediate stage of turf, blessing the countryman with
his usual supply of fuel, free of charge. One can see this
turf bog stretching on and on for miles and miles, a melancholy grayness broken only by the black trenches which
men have been cutting, *e.g.,* the Bog of Allen, which
starts almost at Naas and only ends at Athlone.

These ancient forests lasted right down to the modern
age. The Ossianic tales prove this, and the way of life
which they conjure up, of hunters living mainly by the
chase. We even read of it in the written record: the immense forest which covered Munster was only finally destroyed at the beginning of the seventeenth century, especially to feed the foundries of the Petty family, the ancestors of the present Lord Lansdowne. There is nothing
to be surprised at in the luxuriance of the trees, in a cli-
mate which is above all oceanic, rainy, equable, and soft;
the same as our own Brittany, but a few degrees colder.
Snow is seldom seen in winter anywhere on the plain; and
the finest days in summer are seldom without a certain
coolness. In the West especially, on the Atlantic coast,

it rains in a way that can really be described as chronic. And this overflowing of the water, combined, as it is, in the fat plains of Tipperary and Kildare, with their rich soil, gives to the Irish spring an explosive force which must be seen to be believed. This produces that great carpet of grass, which can grow to a height of eighteen inches in a few days; thence the name, which has been justified a thousand times, of The Emerald Isle; thence those fine horses, with their great bones full of iron, the best hunters in the world; and thence, if the observation may be allowed, the beautiful girls of Limerick.

One should remember that such a land is pastoral rather than agricultural. In the days before the war made tillage obligatory, whole counties were laid down to grass, and the inhabitants lived in lordly ease, "sitting on the ditch and watching the grass grow." From the most ancient time the riches of Ireland have been in its cattle. Maeve and Ailill, the king and queen of the *Tain Bo,* the Irish *Iliad,* count up their treasures in terms of cattle; and when Carew, in the sixteenth century, wished to have done with the men of Munster, he simply destroyed their herds. But the pastoral life is one of leisure; from this comes that lazy, easy way which is handed on from generation to generation, and certain features which strike one in this people, the slower cadence of their life, which is still so to say rural, a certain happy indolence, a habit of taking things easily which is at times almost oriental, a sense of confidence that a benevolent God will continue to clothe the lilies: the carefree ways of herdsmen who have never lacked for grass. And then, long periods of leisure make for a contemplative outlook; now, this moist northern atmosphere brings out vivid, beautiful colors, the gold of the gorse, the purple of the heather, the velvety blue of the distant peaks; and the sea above all,

when the breeze collects and scatters the mist, produces
visions which are as fantastic as they are fugitive, islands
which are half seen and suddenly disappear, illusions,
spells, magic. May not all this help to account for the
fact that Irish thought is inclined to be dreamy, to delight
in the mysterious and the incredible?

Finally, the truly Gaelic way of life was exclusively
rural, and such is the true Gaelic tradition. There were
no towns before the Viking invasion. The people were
scattered, as indeed are the small cottages on the slopes
of the hills to this day. And the social units were also
scattered, very numerous and small, divided up and
firmly anchored in their tribalism. This dispersion, this
taste for seclusion is to be found through the whole of
Irish history in a lack of cohesion, in hatred or at least
ignorance of what is meant by unity. At the same time
there is the narrow family community, in which each one
has known each other from all eternity, with ranks whose
boundaries are fixed with extreme rigor, while genealogies and blood relationship acquire an undisputed importance, ways of thinking which still survive almost intact, anyway in country districts. No society has such a
natural hierarchy as that of the Irish countryside; the
land, the big house, the fine cattle without number, these
are the riches which are valued, and they alone, if they
date from ancient times, give the right to be considered a
"county family." This implicit trust in hereditary values is
to be found throughout Irish history, sometimes to the
extent of being a curse.

Finally, if we would paint a picture of this land, let us
not forget her place on the map. The effect of distance
should be noted; not only is she apart from the continent, but she is far away, cast off, so to speak, in the
open sea, "the nearest parish being America." To the

east, between the continent of Europe and herself, lies the great neighboring island like a wall sheltering her, but at the same time like a mask which precluded many a useful intercourse. This situation has both its advantages and its disadvantages; sometimes (in the days of the Romans and during the last two great wars), it has served as a protection from invasions or from the Barbarians; sometimes, owing to lack of contacts, it has been the cause of outmoded ways of thought and technique. Being at the far end of the pool, Ireland is the last to feel the impact of the waves. This it is, I think, which explains the innate spirit of conservatism, the force of custom and tradition, in this little Atlantic community. Ireland is definitely archaic, and that is not the least of her charms. Changes are only accepted when it seems worth while, the heritage of the old days is considered to be better, as such, and therefore honored. Folklore still crops out everywhere. When St. Patrick wished to test the wisdom of the wise men, he led them from tomb to tomb, asking of them the names, the forefathers, and the great deeds of the old people who lay there. In short, owing to the isolation of the human element, an isolation which is due partly to the dispersion of their dwellings in the countryside, partly to the geographical exile of the island, Ireland is certain, like Brittany and for the same reasons, which in this case are even more powerful, to be slow in her evolution, being held back by the past. There can be no country in Europe where one will find so many survivals of the ancient world, still emerging and surviving, while elsewhere they have vanished.

Chapter 2. The Origins

In the beginning, Ireland was virgin and empty land.
Shortly after the Flood, Partholan, coming from the East,
brought the first colony, which after a few centuries was
destroyed by an epidemic, not one man surviving. Then
came Nemed and his followers, natives of Scythia, who
were constantly harassed by the Fomorians, pirates from
the sea, and their king Balor the Cyclop, so that they
eventually abandoned the country. Two hundred years
later, a band of Nemedians, the Fir Bolg, returned from
Greece and took possession; thirty-six years later, however, they in turn were attacked by a second wave of
Nemedians, the Tuatha De Danann, or people of the goddess Dana, who were skilled in the magic arts; they were
conquered in the battle of Moytura and reduced for ever
to a semi-servile or at least a plebeian condition. Finally,
about the time of Alexander, the three sons of Miledh—
Heremon, Heber and Ir—arrived from Spain and subdued the divine Tuatha De Danann in the battle of Tailltiu. It was not difficult to establish a connection between
the name of Miledh and the somewhat flattering claim of
having a Milesian origin, and this was readily done.

These nursery tales have more than a folklore value.
They were made to synchronize with the biblical compu-
tation, and integrated into a so-called universal history
round about the twelfth century by the authors of the
Book of Invasions; they were accepted as true all through
the Middle Ages, and even later, and this is where their
importance lies. There was no great princely house which
did not allege, by means of some juggling on the part of

its genealogists, that it went back to Milesian times, and on this it would base its claims. It is nowadays difficult to pick out any element in these fables on which one can rely, and at its best the choice will be no more than a surmise. The glimpses one can obtain, mainly through archaelogical exploration, of those races who have remained mute—I mean, who left no written records—are, as everywhere else, traces of prehistoric man, using first split and then polished stone. There then appears a small dark people (the Fir Bolg?), of Mediterranean origin, as is proved by the distribution of megaliths bearing witness to a common culture, which are so often to be found in Ireland, and also in the European area all along the coasts of France and Spain, and as far as Malta. About the middle of the fourth century B.C., the Gaedhil or Gaels, coming from Gaul or Galicia, quickly subjugated the previous inhabitants. The latter had only bronze, while these had iron. They spoke a language not far removed from Latin. They were cousins, not brothers, of those who about the same time conquered the great neighboring island of Britain: they were "Q-Celts," while the others (such as the Gauls) were "P-Celts": which means that they said *ceathair* and not *pedwar*. They were tall in stature, with fresh complexions, reddish-brown hair, and warlike characters; they lost no time in imposing their military aristocracy, their language, and their culture on the aboriginal population. In the North they met with the Picts (painted or tattooed men?), who were the *Pretanoi* of the Greek authors (hence Britons and Britain), the *Qreteni* or *Cruithni* of the Gaelic annals. In the South they found the *Erainn*, the chief tribe of Munster which was to give its name to the country, Eire, Iwerddon, Ierne, Hibernia, according to the various idioms.

After their victory at Tailltiu, the easygoing Gaels came to terms with the conquered. The Children of Dana were to live in their magic palaces underground, while they took to the pleasant hills, forests, and rivers of Ireland. What this legend probably means is that the newcomers combined their traditions with those of the natives. They certainly brought their own gods with them, such as Lug of the Long Hand, Nuadu of the Silver Hand (the poor fellow lost his hand at the battle of Moytura), or Esus with the Three Cranes, as is attested in Gaul by the altar of Cluny; but they adopted Angus Og, "the Young," who lives beneath the huge hollow tumuli of the Boyne Valley, and the Dagda, and finally Dana, the mother of the gods, all of whom belonged to the local pantheon. The Children of Dana, by dint of living in their underground homes, became confused with the people of the fairies, animist deities of immemorial antiquity, whom the peasants timidly try to coax down to the present day by giving them a euphemistic name: "the good people."

The Druids or Seers (prefix dru+id, an Indo-European root, to be compared with the Latin *video,* and the Greek *idein*) seem to have been not so much a religious authority or a clergy as a college of "wise men," versed in all knowledge, especially in prophecy and witchcraft; no warrior would dare to challenge the wonders which they could produce at will, supernatural mists and magical transformations. They seem to have something to do with the *geis,* a magical injunction or prohibition which was also a matter of honor and by which they would often bind kings and heroes. They were to leave, as in Gaul, no written memorial, either because a taboo forbade them to transmit a hermetic tradition except by word of mouth, or else because the *Ogham* then in use was too slow and cumbersome to produce any text longer than the few words of a tumular inscription.[1] The Druids, who fell into decay after the time of St. Patrick, may then have become merged with the *Filidh*, who were to survive as long as Gaelic civilization itself. These latter were poets, and, as is always the case with the primitive *vates*, wizards and thaumaturges and medicine men as well; not only could their satire inflict deadly dishonor on their victims, but they could also afflict them with pustules of a magical nature; being dreaded by all, they were able to make exorbitant demands on the most powerful princes.

Authority lay in the hands of one man, whether patriarch or king; and seeing that monarchy was so rare among the Celts of the continent, it is possible that in this case it was borrowed from the aboriginal inhabitants. A large number of *tuatha* or tribes—about a hundred in all —each had their petty king, and it is said that these can still be recognized in the modern baronies. Above these, the provincial kings ruled over the "Five Fifths" of Ireland, Ulster, Munster, Connaught, and the two Leinsters, north and south. There was no central authority. Ulster, which reached as far south as the Boyne and seems to have been easily the most powerful of the Five, *ipso facto* incited the others to form a coalition.

In this Gaelic society, women had an unusual and superior position, when compared with the perpetual tutelage imposed on them in Mediterranean law. They were queens in their own right, and led their troops into battle, as did the Maeve of Irish legend and the Boadicea of Tacitus. One even seems to discover traces of matriarchy, as, for example, in the fact that certain names mean "son of the

[1] Based on the Latin alphabet, Ogham writing consists of perpendicular or oblique marks, varying from one to five, and traced on either side of a central ridge. The first Irish inscription to be found in Roman characters seems to date from the seventh century (F, Henry, *Irish Sculpture*).

mother" and not of the father. The armed forces were a
medley of levies, possibly backed by mercenaries, and in
which anyway each hero fought his own battle independ-
ently. Their weapons were the spear and the sword, which
they still wielded from the height of a chariot, as did the
Achaean and Hittite warriors and the Caledonians of
Agricola. Their love of magnificent clothes, and especially
of speckled designs, is to be found in many a flattering
description even though these may be no more than poetic
fancies.

Perhaps one of the few glimpses we can obtain of this
mist-girded world is in the Táin Bó, or poem about The
Search for the Bull, which is said to depict the beginning
of the Christian era. Queen Maeve, who when in bed had
been comparing her riches with those of her husband
Aïlill, discovered that he possessed a bull far finer than
any of hers. She was much vexed, and resolved to send
a request for the Bay Bull of Cooley in Ulster, but met
with a refusal; so she launched an attack at the head of the
rest of Ireland. Now, the warriors in Ulster were kept
back far from the field of battle by an annual sickness,
brought about by magic. Cuchulainn alone (a small dark
man—Pict or Celt?) halted the invasion at the ford by a
series of single combats, until, when he was exhausted
and covered with wounds, his divine father, Lug of the
Long Hand, at last came to his assistance. However, having recovered from their long period of weakness, the
men of Ulster came to the rescue. The battle of Ilgairech
began. After incredible acts of valor on the part of
Cuchulainn, Maeve was defeated. She retreated, taking
the Bay Bull with her as a trophy; but when the Bay saw
the White Bull, Aïlill's treasure, the two beasts attacked
each other with such fury that they killed each other, and

the whole of Ireland was covered with their bleeding remains.

In this tale we find once more the Five Fifths, the heroic ideal, the female sovereign, the chariot, the splendid dress of many colors, and that confused mythology in which one would search in vain for a definite pantheon. Who is Cuchulainn? A mortal, a Pict? Or else a god, since he is in fact the son of Lug, and not of an earthly father? In the heat of the battle the small dark man grows into a meteoric wonder: would he be the winter sun, escaping from the clouds and flooding the sky with its light? What are the two horses, the Black and the Gray, which are led by Leg the charioteer? What are the two bulls, the Bay and the White? Are they day and night?

And Finn, the hero of the other Irish epic, the captain of the Fianna defenders of Ireland, in whom people have for a long time hoped to find an historical or semi-historical personality, is no more safe. . . . When analyzed, there only remains a supernatural figure, that of a seer who scans the future by means of divination through his thumb, a sort of hunter-god and prophet. His rival Goll (the One-eyed) is perhaps another avatar of the luminary of the world. And whilst he is an enemy of the Fomore Balor, he is perhaps, under another name, the same as this Balor of the Seven Eyelids, who, if any foolish man were to be so bold as to lift the seventh eyelid, with one burning look would set fire to the green plains of Ireland. Are these the scarcely recognizable vestiges of some worship of the sun, three quarters of which have now fallen into oblivion?

Chapter 3. Christian Ireland

The first centuries of the Christian era saw the West of
Ireland slowly rising to preeminence—one hesitates to
say hegemony. Ulster seemed to be in a state of con-
tinual decline. Conn of the Hundred Battles—who gave
his name to the Province of Connacht—advanced beyond the ancient capital, Rath Croghan in Roscommon,
and established his own people beyond the Shannon at
Uisnech. He pushed on towards the East and installed
himself at Tara; this was from then onwards the symbolic
capital of Ireland. He then founded the kingdom of
Midhe (*anglice* Meath), which replaced on the Boyne
the former kingdom of North Leinster. Clashing in the
South with Eoghan Mór, surnamed Mogh Nuadat (= a
worshiper of the god Nuadu), he fixed their respective
domains by the line of central hills running from Dublin
to Galway, and the memory of this fresh division, the
Half of Mogh and the Half of Conn, was to be perpetuated in the language throughout the ages. He himself assumed for the first time the dignity—for it was little more
—of High King or Ard Rí; it was retained by his descendants, Dal Cuinn or the Race of Conn, for eight centuries, down to 1022.

His grandson, Cormac Mac Art, instituted the annual
assemblies of Tara, or Tailtiu, which were at the same
time parliaments, fairs, and olympiads, in which the cultural, if not the political, unity of the country was af-
firmed. Niall of the Nine Hostages (380-405) brought
the race of Conn to the height of its expansion. Fifty
years earlier, three princes of the same blood, driving
Ulster back past her last defense, the "Wall of the Black

Pig," had cut off from her the state of Airghialla or Oriel (=Vassals of the East). Two of his sons, Eoghan and Conall, now invaded Ulster from the northwest and occupied there the fort of Ailech, which gave its name to the new state. At that moment, then, Ireland consisted of seven kingdoms—Connacht, Munster, and Leinster, which were original; Midhe, Oriel, Ailech, which were new, and Ulaidh on the Antrim coast, which was all that remained of the ancient Ulster. Eoghan (*anglice* Owen) and Conall shared their conquests between them, one founding the dynasty of Tirone (= land of Owen) the other that of Tirconaill, and their posterity was to reign there till the dawn of the seventeenth century. This branch of the Children of Niall, or Ui Neill, allied to other Ui Neill who reigned in Midhe, finally snatched from Connacht the dignity of High King held by Aïlill, who was conquered and killed at the Battle of Ocha (483); after which, for five centuries, the crown, by a curious system, alternated between the two houses, the Ui Neill of Ailech or the North, and the Ui Neill of Midhe or the South.

But there was more than this: the Gaels crossed the water. It was the age when the Roman Empire was falling to pieces, and the legions were leaving the neighboring island of Britain; This Britain was now assailed on the East by the Teutonic tribes, who gave it the name of England. The Gaels colonized the west coast in considerable numbers and made a lasting foundation of the kingdom of Argyle (Oir Ghaedhil = Gaels of the West); they imposed their name on Scotland, for in the ancient texts the word *Scot* always refers to Irishmen. This advance was to have the greatest influence on the later development of the larger island, for in the meanwhile Ireland had become Christian.

St. Patrick, the National Apostle, becomes, according to the latest research, a more than ever nebulous figure: one scholar has recently even suggested that there were in fact two Patricks, who later became telescoped into one. The traditional history gives a most attractive picture of him; he seems to have been highly civilized, charitable, humane, diplomatic, and to have brought about his spiritual and moral revolution practically without any violence. A Roman citizen, born at Bannaven Taberniae (?), Patricius the son of Calpurnius was at the age of sixteen carried away in one of those raids by which the Gaels recruited their slaves, for whom Bristol was for several centuries the market. For six years he was a swineherd, after which he escaped and went to Auxerre to study under St. Germain, for he dreamed of evangelizing the pagan masters whom he had served; he came back as bishop in 432 and died at an advanced age in 461, having completed the chief part of his task.

Being a Roman, taught in Gaul, Patrick's aim was to found a church on Roman lines, with a strict hierarchy, bishops ruling over vast dioceses and governing priests and monks side by side, who would prove pious sons of Rome, the fountainhead, the supreme authority in dogma and in discipline. He named four disciples for the four sees that he founded, and the best loved of them, Benen the Irishman, for his own see of Armagh. But this fine "imperial" order cut across the economic, social, and political conditions of the country, which had no towns or major means of communication and was split up into autonomous and self-sufficing tribes, having at the same time a deep love for its national originality. There are even some who think that the development of affairs may be accounted for by contacts with the churches of the East, and comparative art certainly points to this. Whatever the reason may be, it is a fact that a church soon grew which was very different in its inspiration from the church of St. Patrick. Monks were more prominent than priests, monasteries generally took the place of dioceses, the abbot rather than the bishop ruled. The hermit life with its solitude, and a strangely excessive form of asceticism, became the ideal of the religious life; the monks tended towards isolation even within their enclosure, as is proved by the large number of tiny sanctuaries, each one made for one cleric and incapable of holding more than twenty faithful. The Irish saints were founders of monasteries, Enda, Finnian, Ciaran, Brendan and Carthach, the creators of Aran Mor, Clonard, Clonmacnois, Clonfert, and Lismore.

Such a state of affairs had both its bright and its reverse side. On the one hand it produced human types endowed with admirable virtues.[2] On the other hand, as the result of this excessive isolation from the world, the very same world was left too much to its guilty and sinful ways. The clergy were too holy, and the laity not holy enough. And then it often happened that these monasteries, having been founded by the pious generosity of some local chieftain, with all the belief of the Gaelic spirit in the rights of blood relationship, the same chieftain soon came to look upon the foundation as his own property, and the line of *coarbs* or successors, would become hereditary. Finally, with the collapse of the empire, the barbarian invasions cut off this small outlying

[2] And with a humor which is the supreme achievement of these virtues. Three Irish monks took refuge in the wilderness, under a vow of silence. At the end of a year, the first ventured to say: "The hermit life is a good one." At the end of two years, the second said: "Yes." At the end of the third, the third monk burst out with: "If one cannot live in peace here, I shall return to the world!"

church from Rome; and then not only was it geographi-
cally eccentric, but it tended towards eccentricity in the
other sense of the word. With the pride and independence which are characteristic of the race, the Gaelic
church clung to certain singularities, not indeed in matters of dogma, but in practices which were entirely its
own, such as a peculiar form of tonsure and a different
date for Easter, to each of which it clung stubbornly.
One can thus understand why it was not the glory of
Patrick, the Roman, which dazzled those early ages, but
that of Columbcille, the Gael.

His life, as written by Adamnan, his ninth successor,
reads like a romance. The "Dove of the Church" was
born in Tirconaill of the royal blood of the Ui Neill. He
went into exile out of remorse, after a war which he
brought about by having surreptitiously copied a precious
psalter; leaving his beloved Derry, he founded the monastery of Iona, from whence, as Abbot of the isles, he set
out to convert the Scotland of his day, divided as it was
between the three races of Gaels, Picts, and Saxons, while
his disciple Aidan, the Abbot of Lindisfarne, succeeded
in two thirds of England. In 575 he was recalled by Aed,
the High King, to attend the Assembly of Drumceat,
which was so exasperated by the exactions of the *filidh*
that it wished to outlaw the whole caste. But if
Columbcille was a cleric, he was also a prince; if he was
an ascetic, he was also a man of letters, an antiquarian,
and a poet: he set out to save his brethren, and laid it
down that from thenceforward every chief, whether of a
tribe or a province, was bound to maintain a royal poet
in honorable circumstances, an *ollamh,* who would act
as bard, genealogist, and chronicler of his house.
Columbcille died, full of years, in 597.

The controversy between the church of Canterbury,

heir of St. Augustine, and the Celtic Christians, heirs of Columbcille, over the date of Easter and the tonsure was going on indefatigably. At the Synod of Whitby (664) Colman, the Abbot of Iona, once more vigorously supported the Irish peculiarities, and as King Oswy gave the decision against him, rather than yield he chose to leave his see and near Galway to go and die, along with his faithful, in a new foundation in Ireland. Iona itself did not yield till 716. It needed Malachy, the spiritual son of St. Bernard, in the XIIth century before the Gaelic church could be finally made to observe the common customs.

Chapter 4. The Golden Age

The Irish monasteries, Clonard, Clonmacnois, Armagh, then later Bangor and Lindisfarne, were centers not only of spiritual, but also of intellectual, life; they were in a sense the universities of their day. Being surrounded in their own country with religious respect, and protected by distance from the great barbarian invasions and the relapse into savagery which they caused, they were the only lights still burning in the night which had come down over the West; for two centuries Ireland, being thus privileged, was truly to be the teacher of Europe. Her widespread fame for learning and piety brought her a host of disciples: according to the tradition, no less than three thousand had gathered round St. Finnian at Clonard, and Armagh was so swarming with English students that it had a special Saxon quarter. The Merovingian king Dagobert possibly was educated at Slane. Travelers would also pay visits; Adamnan, of Iona,

wrote his *De Locis Sanctis* at the dictation of a bishop of
Gaul, one Asculf, who had returned from the Holy Land.
Theological speculation was no doubt the most important
study, to which the name of John Scotus Eriugena (this
name says twice that he was an Irishman) bears witness;
but it was nevertheless a monk, Dicuil, who composed a
universal geography, *De mensura orbis terrarum,* while
Fergal, the Abbot of Aghadoe, was even in those far-off
days teaching that the earth is round.

The intellectual advance which Ireland felt she had
on a barbaric Europe, and the charity with which she
was animated for the peoples who had sunk or were still
pagan, filled her with zeal. She applied herself eagerly to
the conquest of minds and souls. In her view the work
of evangelization must go *pari passu* with the bringing
of light. The Carolingian renaissance owed much to her.
The bold theologian John Scotus taught for twenty-five
years in the schools of Laon, under Charles the Bald.
Fergal of Aghadoe is the same as Virgil, Bishop of Salz-
burg, whose dangerous teaching about the antipodes did
not prevent him from being later canonized by the Holy
See. Along with the men of learning, there were mis-
sionaries and their missions: St. Fursa at Peronne
(*Peronna Scotorum*), St. Fiacre near Meaux, St. Cilian
at Wurzburg, and one will find others as far away as
Taranto and Kiev. The most famous of all was St.
Columban, who "in order to win a heavenly fatherland
through exile," left Bangor and having founded Luxeuil
in Gaul, was then deported by the wicked King Thierry
II; instead of returning to Ireland he escaped, and having
left his disciple, St. Gall, at Reichenau, Switzerland, fin-
ished his course in what was to be the best-known house
of his order, Bobbio, in 615. The Ireland of those days

had every cause to be known as "the isle of saints and scholars."

A fact which contributed to her spiritual expansion was that with the coming of Christianity Latin had become her second language. It went near to being the first: a cleric such as Adamnan, for instance, had nothing but disdain for the vernacular tongue, and Gaelic was only able to maintain its position through the love borne it by the *filidh*. But Irish thought was eventually able to find its way to all parts of the known world, under the wing of Latin, the universal language. Ireland took her cultural vocabulary also from Christianity and from Rome, as her words for *priest, book, to write,* etc. testify, and from Rome she also received her form of writing, that lovely *oncial* which has survived in the Gaelic characters down to our own day.

Besides, calligraphy was one of the arts most diligently cultivated in the monasteries; the *scriptorium* was one of the essential parts of a monastery, and was generally given a special place between the vaulting and the roof; the reproduction of manuscripts was regarded as an essential work. This had a twofold result: on the one hand, as the profane authors were revered almost as much as the sacred, the Irish scribes have preserved for us a considerable number of their classical works; on the other hand, they were able to create the most astonishing wonders. The excellence of the Irish handwriting was admitted and manuscripts *scotice scripti* were held to be of the finest quality; and, when Irish art passed from pure calligraphy to illumination, it produced masterpieces which have never been surpassed, such as the Book of Durrow, the Book of Lindisfarne, and, above all, the incomparable Book of Kells—all of which, it should be noted, were the work of foundations connected with the name of Columbcille.

This art, which shows how infinitely the Irish were ahead of their time, whether on vellum or in metal, in the pages of the Book of Kells or on the Ardagh Chalice, rests on a system of ever-recurring and interlacing lines. One would show a complete lack of understanding of its character if one accused it of awkwardness or of wild fantasy. It has, in contrast to Greek art, no desire to represent things or beings. It is a very ancient form of art, which certainly goes back to prehistoric tradition, and when, as then, it is serving pious ends, unconsciously remains packed with ancient Celtic gods and Germanic animals. Are we amazed at its fondness for the play of lines pure and simple? That is because it is of magical origin. It is a question of giving to a thing, a lump of stone, for instance, the virtue of a protective incantation by decorating it with a suitable pattern, while at the same time one is afraid to alter its shape. As the intention is of an abstract kind, any allusion which makes it intelligible is held to be sufficient, and all realist preoccupations are set aside. That is why every figure, whether human or animal, is designed not so much to recall the special animal or man, but rather so that it shall spread out and then turn and wind backwards and forwards, in order to fulfil its function and its place in the design as conceived *a priori*.

The aim is to suggest things and beings without portraying them exactly, and thus is expressed the Irish instinct which keeps the ornament in a delicate and precarious balance between geometry and figuration, in a state of constant oscillation, from which it derives its quality of evasive fluidity. An arabesque finishes up as foliage, a spiral as the jaws of a monster. And this same character is linked with another aspect of Gaelic thought which is frequently to be found in the tales: a supernatural conception of the world, a belief in the instability of forms and in the transmutation of beings, a passion for the improbable. If an animal half becomes a plant or if a curve bursts into leaf what is there surprising in that? They do not need to be real, it is enough that they should be possible. And the secret of this truly great and refined art is a very subtle one, it is to endow these monsters with life, to convince us that they really exist.

The effect is obtained by the use of extremely studied and conscious methods, such as giving an impression of complexity by the use of elements which in themselves are simple and clear, or else by tracing harmonious curves which only a minute examination will disclose as being dissimilar. But one should note that this effect, which has in truth the quality of an incantation, of a decorative litany, is produced by the constant coiling back of these forms on themselves, by repetition and persistence, the everlasting "return" giving a sense of supernatural possession. It is also remarkable, though perhaps not surprising, that Gaelic music, poetry, and prosody, arts which are all related to one another, reveal the same instinct: the old traditional airs all end with the same melancholy clause, in which the same note is repeated three times, while the poems delight in parallel antitheses, arranged in distichs and triads; the verse is woven to and fro, with a studied refinement that is at times alarming in its ingenuity, and with internal or concluding assonances, alliterations, and the constant recall of the same sounds, whether of vowels or consonants. A text will illustrate better than any commentary the formal perfection and the polished charm which this method was capable of attaining in those ancient times.

I and Pangur Ban, my cat,
'Tis a like task we are at;
Hunting mice is his delight,
Hunting words I sit all night.

Better far than praise of men
'Tis to sit with book and pen;
Pangur bears me no ill will,
He too plies his simple skill.

'Tis a merry thing to see
At our tasks how glad are we,
When at home we sit and find
Entertainment to our mind.

Oftentimes a mouse will stray
In the hero Pangur's way;
Oftentimes my keen thought set
Takes a meaning in its net.

'Gainst the wall he sets his eye
Full and fierce and sharp and sly;
'Gainst the wall of knowledge I
All my little wisdom try.

When a mouse darts from its den,
O how glad is Pangur then!
O what gladness do I prove
When I solve the doubts I love!

So in peace our tasks we ply,
Pangur Ban, my cat and I;
In our arts we find our bliss,
I have mine and he has his.

> *Practice every day has made*
> *Pangur perfect in his trade;*
> *I get wisdom day and night*
> *Turning darkness into light.*

This delightful flash of wit, which must have beguiled the tedium of some Irish scribe, is to be found in the margin of an eighth-century psalter,[3] a hundred years before the French language peeps out for the first time in the *Serments de Strasbourg.*

Chapter 5. Brian Boru

One reads, in the *Annals of the Four Masters,* for the year 795, "The island of Rathlinn was burnt to ashes; its sanctuaries destroyed and plundered." This was the arrival of the Danes upon the scene.[4] Ireland provided them with an ideal country for pillage, being deeply penetrated by gulfs and rivers, with no spot in it far from the sea; it had no organized forces and was covered with wealthy monasteries. Their coats of mail, their axes and their swords of well-tempered steel gave them complete technical superiority. They loitered for a long time in England and Scotland, where they annexed the Orkneys, the Shetlands, the Hebrides, and the Isle of Man, while in Ireland they attempted no more than coastal raids. It

[3] I quote Robin Flower's translation, from *Poems and Translations,* pp. 129-130.
[4] *Danes* is the generic name by which the English language means the Scandinavian sea kings, who were, however, mainly Norwegian. I use it for the sake of convenience, and keep the name of Norman for the twelfth-century invaders, who came from the French Normandy. The Gaelic name for the Danes is Lochlannaigh.

was not till 830 that Torgeist, a Viking chief, tried to establish his dominion over the land itself; he set himself at Armagh, which he plundered, while claiming at the same time that he was its Abbot, and we find his wife, Ota, who was a seer, giving out her oracles sitting on the high altar at Clonmacnois (841). Scandinavian savagery quickly infected, like some contagion, the native princes: among those who, each in his turn, laid waste Clonmacnois, one finds a certain Phelim, King of Cashel, who is described as "bishop and scribe"! The fact is that, instead of uniting against the attack from without, they were exhausting each other in wrangles for the various kingdoms, or for the title of Ard Rí. Now and then an ephemeral reaction was launched against the foreign aggressor, as when the High King Maelsechlainn captured Torgeist and had him drowned.

About that time the Danes were concentrating their efforts against the England of Alfred the Great. Not that they left Ireland completely; they founded scattered coastal settlements, which at first were only ports of call and markets, but later became stockaded enclosures in which they could run their ships aground, and finally they grew into towns—the first to be seen in the Gaelic land. Dublin (Dubh Linn—The Black Pond), which arose by the ford that commands the Liffey, was founded in 841, lost and recaptured, and from then onwards was the capital of a kingdom over which reigned the sons of the King of Norway, Ivar and Olaf. Other settlements followed, Wicklow, Arklow, Wexford, Waterford, Cork, Limerick, Carlingford. After the death of Ivar in 873 Ireland had a respite for forty years, till about 915. It was not long before the two races were being drawn together by marriages, children of a mixed race were born, and Danes were to be found gradually adopting Christian ways; this, however, did not exclude them from business as usual. It is difficult to tell how it came about, but parties were formed through temporary alliances, and Danish-Irish would be setting out to attack Irish-Danish. The confusion then grew worse, because of the rule being broken by which the Ui Neill of the North and South held the supreme authority alternately. And, furthermore, Olaf of the Sandals, a descendant of Ivar, and King of Dublin, subjected the province of Midhe to a "Babylonish captivity." One can well understand the petition which the liturgy of those days added to the litanies: *A furore Normannorum, libera nos, Domine!* Also the monk's timorous stanza:

> *Fierce is the wind this night*
> *Brushing back the white mane of the billow;*
> *This night the savage warriors of Norway*
> *Will not sail across the Irish sea.*

It was, however, a King of Midhe, Maelsechlainn II, who, at the battle of Tara, broke the might of Olaf and the Foreigners of Dublin and immediately became High King (980). Another star was meanwhile rising in the South. Munster, or the kingdom of Cashel, was burdened with the tribute which it was forced to pay to Ivar, the Danish King of Limerick; its ancient dynasty, that of the sons of Eoghan, had yielded to the new masters. Two brothers, Mahon and Brian, who were petty kings of the tiny state of Dal Cais on the borders of Claire, rose against Ivar, and Mahon ruled without opposition at Cashel for many years. Then he was captured by Ivar and put to death. Brian, who alone was left, fought and killed Ivar and thus became King of Cashel, at the expense of the Eoghanachta, who were the lawful princes; this was his first usurpation (976). A few years later, profiting by some internal quarrels, he overcame the neighboring province of Leinster and Dublin itself, and they agreed to be his vassals.

Maelsechlainn, who with reason distrusted this rising power, had tried to break it, but in vain. He had to recognize Brian as the independent king of the South, or the half of Mogh; this was the second usurpation. So unstable a dyarchy could not last, and at Tara in 1002 Brian called upon the other to yield the primacy to him, and, abandoned by his allies, the Ui Neill of the North, Maelsechlainn gave way; the Ui Neill, after six hundred years, were clearing out and Brian seized the supreme dignity; this was the third usurpation. He was now Brian Boru, Brian of the Tributes, who as lord paramount could levy the tribute of homage and take hostages from the whole land of Ireland.

That he was conscious of having a mission is clearly shown by the colophon which he caused to be added to the *Book of Armagh* by his scribe, Maelsuthain, and which describes him as Emperor of Ireland, *Imperator Scotorum*. His mind was haunted by the memory of the Roman Caesar and the later Charlemagne, and of the benefits which had been brought by the peace they imposed. He would give to the country that which in those days was unheard of, a state, an order, a head. He would reign. He had already reduced the proud Ui Neill of the North to obedience. He restored the Assembly of Tailtiu, which had been in abeyance for eighty years. And then he set about rebuilding monasteries and schools, buying books abroad to replace those which had been burnt or lost; he recognized Armagh as the primatial see, and imposed the benefit of his rule on all sides.

A fury cut across his plans, a certain Gormflaith, the sister of Maelmora, the King of Leinster, who had in turn been the wife of Olaf, of Maelsechlainn, and finally of Brian Boru. Having been repudiated by him, she first stirred up her brother against him, along with the King of Dublin, Sitric of the Silken Beard, a son whom she had borne to Olaf. Too weak on their own, the pair called in the Danes from outside; it was the time when they were masters of England, after the victories of Sweyn and Canute, and they were thinking of securing Ireland, too. They came from far and wide, from the Isle of Man and from the Hebrides, from the Orkneys and even from the Baltic; Gormflaith had promised her hand in marriage to Sigurd, the Iarl of the Orkneys, along with the kingdom of Ireland. Brian arrived from his fortress of Kincora, with his old well-tried contingents. The battle began on Good Friday, April 23, 1014, just outside the walls of Dublin. Sigurd commanded the Danes; Murchadh, the son of Brian, the men of Munster And Connacht. The old king was watching, for he was too aged to fight, and Sitric too was looking on from the top of the ramparts. The fighting began at dawn. Towards the end of the day the routed Danes, being cut off from their ships by the high tide, were being drowned by the hundreds; Siguard and Maelmora were dead, and so was Murchadh; his sixteen-year-old son, Turloch, was drowned, along with a Dane whom he had hunted to death, the pair of them each holding the other by the hair. During his flight a Manx chief, Brodir, recognized Brian in the door of his tent, and split his head open with a blow from his axe. No matter! Danish power was at an end (1014).

The body of the emperor was carried in state to the holy land of Armagh; but his achievements were already crumbling away, owing to the centrifugal and anarchical traditions, which came naturally to the clans. The con-

querors, when they returned home, were challenged and
then attacked by the men of Ossory. The idea of a High
King who truly ruled came to an end. All that remained
of the example of Brian Boru was the proof, doubtful
and dangerous though it was, that it was possible for an
upstart to claim everything. The seven kingdoms had in
fact regained their independence. Maelsechlainn II became Ard Rí again until his death (1022). After him
this dignity was held, though with difficulty, by the children of Brian, the O'Briens, until their defeat at Moy
Cora, when they were forced back into obscurity (1103).
A new dynasty then arose, the O'Connors of Connacht,
Turloch (1106-1156), then Rory, his son, who was to
be last High King of Ireland.

A strange destiny was that of Brian Boru; a kind of
Bonaparte on a small scale, as much by his brilliant triumphs and by the firmness of his rule, as by the sudden
collapse of his system, an imperial figure who did not miss
even the poetic privilege of falling at the very moment of
victory, which epic event inspired the famous manuscript,
The War of the Gael and the Gall (*Gall* = foreigners).
The only valid excuse for his usurpation would have
been to have left his country with a legacy of peace and
order; but as soon as he was dead, both of these vanished
as well. And this was the moment when a new threat was
rising on the horizon, that of the Normans of Normandy,
who had recently annexed Sicily and England, conquered
Wales, and were giving every indication that they did
not intend to stop there.

Chapter 6. The Norman Conquest

A certain Dermot mac Murrough had been King of Leinster and of the Foreigners of Dublin (the Danes) since 1126. Maelmora had been succeeded by a Dermot, then by his son Murcadh, then by the descendants of Murchadh, or mac Murrough. This Dermot was altogether a man of his age, fond of poetry and of fine tales (the famous *Book of Leinster* was compiled for him round about the year 1150), yet capable of the most amazing savagery, as when he caused seventeen of his opponents to be blinded—and worse. In 1141 he suppressed a rising of petty kings, who were his vassals, in an abominable way, and in 1151, in a period of general tumult, he carried off the beautiful Dervorgilla, the wife of O'Rourke the King of Breffni (thus the Gaelic saga also has its Helen). O'Rourke's reply, which was no doubt the product of partisan spirit rather than outraged honor, came in 1166, when he backed a second revolt of the chiefs of Leinster; Dermot was abandoned by all and had to flee. We know what happened and what followed from a French epic, *Chanson de Dermot et du Comte*.

Dermot, who was a man of resource, did not lose his head; he could summon foreign help. He set out to find Henry II of England, who was somewhere in Aquitania; the latter was interested, and granted him letters patent authorizing him to raise men from among his people. The land of Wales, which was as yet scarcely subdued, and the Marches of which were a very warlike area, was swarming with Normans who were full of the spirit of adventure and greed; they were, too, alarmed at the secret hostility which they knew that Henry had for men

like themselves, who owed everything to King Stephen
and only asked for one thing, the chance of freebooting.
Numbers of them were descended from Nesta, a Welsh
princess, who, by her legitimate marriage with Gerald of
Windsor, and her illegitimate connection with Henry I
and with Stephen, the High Constable of Cardigan, had
produced the swarming race of Fitzgeralds, FitzHenrys
and FitzStephens. In 1167 Dermot returned with some
of them, was beaten and came to terms. In 1169 he was
joined by ninety of them, along with three hundred arch-
ers, and this time nobody was able to dislodge them from
their stronghold at Baginbun. In the following year Richard, Earl of Pembroke, nicknamed Strongbow, having
being promised Aoife, Dermot's daughter, in marriage,
with the succession to the kingdom of Leinster, landed
with a thousand men-at-arms. With this force he was
able to seize Waterford, to behead the Danish Count
Sitric, and to marry Aoife. Dublin was taken by surprise, and Count Asgall fled. After this Dermot died.
Strongbow, who was now King of Leinster, was besieged
in Dublin by the High King, Rory O'Connor; his condition was desperate, till the besieging enemy were surprised and dispersed by a sudden sortie of six hundred
horsemen. At this point Strongbow's men considered that
they were capable of conquering Ireland on their own.

And perhaps they were, for, numbers apart, they had
all the advantages on their side. In contrast to the turbu-
lent Irish levies they were professionals, trained and
disciplined, and knew no virtue except that of courage.
And they must conquer or die, for they knew that in
England they were outlaws, even more than here. Besides, how could the Gaelic *kern,* who had neither armor
nor helmet, stand up against these horsemen clad in
mail, and the quick-firing bows? It was as if he were

faced with machine guns or tanks. After the victory of
Thurles the Irish announced, as if it was a marvel, that
four of these men-at-arms had been killed. The invaders
had the same superiority in fortification: as they advanced, they made their advance secure with stone castles
like those with which Foulques Nerra had covered the
Loire, fortresses which could never be taken by the simple native ways and means. Finally, their Norman astute-
ness would not shrink from the use of any weapon,
whether that of broken promises or of treason. They were
thus able to score triumphs that were not only easy but
lasting.

Meanwhile Henry was returning as fast as possible
from the continent; he had already reached Pembroke,
accompanied by four thousand men; he distrusted these
gentlemen of fortune, who were probably thinking about
how they could carve out a kingdom for themselves just
when it was his intention that they should pull the chest-
nuts out of the fire for his benefit. Strongbow, whose father had been belabored by the rough Plantagenet fist,
had a legal mind, and preferred to be a baron in security
rather than a king by chance: he submitted. From then onwards things went easily. In Waterford Henry confirmed
the liberties of the Danish inhabitants and kept the city
for himself; he did the same with every port. When there,
he received the homage of some Gaelic princes, and
moved on to Dublin, where he spent the winter; here he
was visited by the other princes, who came to kiss him on
the shoulder, except for the High King Rory and the
chiefs of the North. He summoned a synod at Cashel at
which the bishops found no difficulty in recognizing him;
it is possible that he held a title from Adrian IV (Break-
speare, the only Englishman ever to be Pope), giving him
power to act as king of the island in the event of his

conquering it, on condition that he should reform the Church[5] and the people, and should restore the payment of Peter's Pence; this would have been the famous Bull *Laudabiliter* (1155) which nobody has ever seen, but which seems to be supported by a certain amount of indirect testimony, and which anyway was never rejected as spurious by Irish tradition. His civilizing mission was confirmed in three letters, still extant, from Pope Alexander III to himself, to the Church, and to the people of Ireland, approving of what had been done (1172). The Plantagenet thus appeared as a lawful prince and an authorized reformer; that, no doubt, is the reason why the bishops accepted him without opposition. The Gaelic chiefs would only have seen in him an even more theoretical Ard Rí than the other, since he was further away, and under the circumstances one homage more or less did not seem to them of much importance. They were soon to be disillusioned.

When he departed, Henry II left behind him his deputy, Hugh de Lacy, as Justiciar of Ireland. The same de Lacy lost no time in awarding to himself the kingdom of Meath, comprising 500,000 acres, at the expense of the O'Melaghlin, and disposing of Tiernan O'Rourke, the King of Breffni, by treachery, during an interview. Meanwhile Strongbow was strengthening his hold in Leinster; in Munster, Fitzgerald was evicting MacCarthy,

[5] Most of this had already been done. St. Malachy, friend of St. Bernard, who wished to be buried in the Irish saint's habit, had already completed the reform of the Irish Church by reducing Gaelic peculiarities to Roman order; St. Malachy journeyed twice to Rome to request the pallium for the Irish archbishops, and had founded at Mellifont the first Cistercian monastery (1142), which was at the same time the first example in Ireland of European architecture. On the other hand there still were outbursts of violence from the local chieftains, which the hierarchy expected Henry to suppress.

and John de Courcy was carving out for himself a
princely domain in Ulster; John Comyn, selected by the
English prelates, succeeded the native Archbishop, St.
Laurence O'Toole, in the see of Dublin. It was becoming
clear that neither homage nor submission would provide
any Gael, whether clerical or lay, with any protection
from the crown; the newcomers intended to take possession of everything, in Church or land; the process of freebooting continued. Furthermore, having been created by
his father "Lord of Ireland," Prince John arrived on the
spot to confirm the plunder. There were, in short, three
initial waves of adventurers: those who arrived first, with
Strongbow, the Fitzgeralds, the Birminghams, and the
Carews; those who came with Henry, the de Lacys, de
Courcys, and others; those who landed with John in
1185, and who were not quite so greedy, the Verduns,
the du Bourgs or de Burgos (Bourkes), and the Theo-
bald Gautiers, the prince's bottlers, who, under the
name of Butler, were to be founders of the powerful
house of Ormond.

There was nothing which could bring together the two
races, the invaders and the invaded: neither language,
since the one spoke French, and the other Gaelic; nor
institutions, since on the one side there was the carefully
worked out scale of feudalism, on the other the vaguely
federal patriarchal tribes; nor juridical conception, with
primogeniture on one hand and limited election on the
other. Nor indeed did they have any common interest;
the Irish, in their unsullied pride, were astounded to find
themselves being robbed, without any pretext, of lands
which their ancestors had possessed from time immemorial, while the Normans looked on them as an inferior
and savage race, in any event without rights, with no
share in the guarantees secured by the law; they looked

with delight at this Cockaigne which was to be had for
the asking, at the ocean of grass and the fat cattle which
would give them riches, power, and glory, and where
from then onwards the natives would have but one place,
that of being *betaghs,* or serfs. It would be an under-
statement to say that each side hated the other; they had
no common meeting ground, they remained unintelligi-
ble to each other. Giraldus Cambrensis, who wrote the
chronicle of those times, speaks of this strange country
as the Other World.

Chapter 7. Ebb and Flow of Norman Feudalism

One would try in vain, in the small space at one's disposal, to follow the irregular rise of the Norman tide.
And it would perhaps be an idle task as well. For three
centuries these transitory states, which expanded and con-
tract like accordions in their movements inwards and out-
wards, as the result of a battle, a marriage, or a succession, only provide the mind with an effect of monotonous
confusion. If one is, however, able to discover some
rhythm, it is that round about the end of the twelfth
century the tide had reached its highest point; from then
onwards, right down to the sixteenth, the ebb gained in
momentum. Why was this?

For a long time the same plot is repeated *ad nauseam:*
there is arbitrary usurpation, often in spite of a plighted
word, there are armed expeditions in order to carry out
evictions, there is the triumph of the Norman technical
skill and the incapacity of the Irish clans to unite or, indeed, to refrain from inviting the foreigners to take part
in their quarrels. Three great houses finally emerge from

among the Norman barons: the Fitzgeralds, of which the younger branch had their possessions in Desmond or southern Munster, and the elder branch in Kildare; the Butlers, who increased their principality of Ormond or Eastern Munster with the addition of Kilkenny, on the dismemberment of Strongbow's fief, when his posterity became extinct in 1240; finally the du Bourgs or de Burgos, also known as the Bourkes, whose lands in Connacht, at the time of the Red Earl, finally reach eastern Ulster, which had come to them as a heritage from the great de Lacy and spanned Ireland from one sea to the other.

The conquest might have been both rapid and lasting if only the foreigners had tried to draw nearer to those upon whom they were preying. But these great nobles, intractable though they might be, did not question their allegiance to the king in London. And this king, who was engaged with other and more important affairs, only adopted a policy of postponement in regard to Ireland, which was sterile and in consequence cruel; he had his fat pullet in the larder, and that was enough for him. He held the ports, and he could land when he wished. No prince thought of contending with him for the island. He had his barons over there who were carrying on the work of conquest as far as they were able, on their own account and at no expense to himself. His line of conduct was to grudge them the wherewithal and now and then to appear in force and rap them over the knuckles, with the sole aim of keeping them in check. But he always remained a *foreign* power, and what is more, a master who was indifferent to the welfare of the country which he claimed as his own. He refused to be King of Ireland.

Awakened by pain, this great disunietd body of Gaelic Ireland shows disconnected reactions of instinct. One can

see it making sporadic efforts towards unity, offering the
crown to Brian O'Neill (1258), to Haakon the King of
Norway (1263), to Edward Bruce, who had come from
Scotland and for a time swept everything before him and
whose reverses and death were merely due to his over-
confidence (1318). One finds it trying to prevent the
wars of succession within the clans by promoting an
original solution, the choice of a *tanist,* to be heir presumptive during the lifetime of the chief; unfortunately,
when the chief died, *tanist* or no *tanist,* ambitions came
into play, and down poured the blows. Thus, Ireland
continued to be devoured alive.

There was a gradual tendency towards a more even
balance between the two forces. The Gaels took to armor
and built castles of stone; at the battle of Athenry, which
they lost, the armor of the dead men was worth a fortune
to the victors. Other factors also intervened, as, for instance, the mixture of bloods. This dates back very far;
in the beginning of the XIIth century Hugh de Lacy
married a daughter of O'Connor the High King; there
were more and more of such marriages, so that before
long there were scarcely any great houses which were altogether Gaelic or altogether Norman. And next, *Hibernia
capta ferum victorem coepit,* Ireland now absorbed her
conquerors. These knights were very few in number in
comparison with the native population, and it was right
that such a sprinkle should become absorbed into it,
just as the Normans of England abandoned their French
language about the year 1360; in Ireland, they took to
the surrounding Gaelic when they renounced the French
of their class. They were soon adopting the Gaelic life
and all its customs, the small harp, the custom of riding
bareback, the maintenance of the seigniorial bard, the
poetry and the music, in fact the whole native tradition.

Just as Ireland had finally absorbed the Danes, so was she now digesting the Normans.

A prince like Gerald FitzGerald, the third Earl of Desmond, left a great name behind him in Gaelic poetry, and again at the time of Cromwell another poet of the Gaels, Pierce Ferriter, revealed his French origin by his patronymic, le Furetier. *Hibernis hiberniores,* according to the famous saying, "more Irish than the Irish themselves," that is what the Normans had become. This is even stressed in the language: the Normans were known in Ireland as "the old foreigners," that is to say, those who had ceased to be so, while the same men were known in England as the "degenerate English."

It was against them and for them, in the hopes of recalling or holding them, that the Statutes of Kilkenny were passed (1367), which were to poison the atmosphere for centuries. These statutes express first fear and then hatred, both of which are eminently sterile. Loyal subjects are forbidden to recognize the native law, *viz.,* the law of the Brehons, to speak Irish, to ride or to dress in the Irish fashion, to adopt the custom of "fosterage," to marry those of Irish blood, all this under penalty of high treason; this is the reflex action of those who feel that the offensive is now turning against them and who do not wish to be driven into the sea. We find the impress of this deeply ingrained fear in the very soil, in the *Pale* (an enclosure with palisade)—a sort of *ager* or *limes* to prevent the raiding of cattle from Norman territory—which was moving backward day by day; at one time it reached the Shannon at Athlone, and now it only enclosed a narrow coastal strip from Dublin to Dundalk—and Dundalk was none too safe!

These Statutes of Kilkenny did not usually weigh very heavily—nobody troubled much about them; ten years

after their promulgation (1388), the same Third Earl
of Desmond sent his son to be brought up by Conor
O'Brien, the brother of the King of Thomond, who became his foster father. Nevertheless, the Statutes continued to be a menace, as a rule in theory rather than in
practice, but hanging over the heads, with the possibility
of the thread being cut at any time: almost one hundred
years later, in 1468, an Earl of Desmond was executed
by order of the Lord Deputy Tibetot for the crime of
having contracted Gaelic alliances. Worse still, the Statutes, by their very spirit, excluded all possibility of an
understanding between the crown and the people of the
island. They define three types of inhabitants: the "loyal"
subjects of the Pale, who are English in language, customs, law, and practice; the "degenerate" English, who
are still subjects, but suspected of having doubtful tendencies, and whom it was considered desirable to recall
to the fold; finally there are the "Irish enemy," who for
this very reason are excluded from all chances of peace
or reconciliation and are without the protection of the
law, pariahs in their own country, condemned either to
disappear or to fight. It is true that the sword usually
remained in its sheath but, whether it was drawn or not,
its point was there.

These "degenerate" English, or "old foreigners," who
formed a kind of intermediate class between the Anglicized Pale of the Lord Justiciar (or Lord Deputy as he
was now called) and the mass of the native inhabitants,
who exactly were they? They were specially represented
by two great families, the Fitzgeralds and the Butlers.
The great Earls of Ulster and Connaught had disappeared, the last Bourke having been assassinated in 1333
out of revenge for an uncle whom he had caused to starve
to death, and the rest of them, in the West, having turned

Gael, abandoned the patronymic of Bourke for the indigenous name of MacWilliam. The Butlers, who had been created Earls of Ormond in 1339, remained loyal for one reason, viz., because they had large possessions in England, but also out of jealousy of the Desmonds. Of the Fitzgerald family, one branch had been Earls of Desmond since 1329, while the others had been made Earls of Kildare in 1316; the latter, being nearer Dublin, played a larger and more direct part in the affairs of the Castle, the former, living farther away, did much as they pleased in their mountains. They held an almost royal rank in their palatinates, with power to create knights and even barons; but as they were too powerful they came under the suspicion of the Crown. Not that they ever thought of repudiating their formal allegiance, of that they seem to have had no idea—provided that this allegiance in no sense detracted from their *de facto* independence; for instance, in order to avenge his brother who had been executed, James Earl of Desmond ravaged the "loyal" lands of Midhe. These great nobles lived in completely Irish style, surrounded by their bards and their harpers, usually choosing places for their establishments outside the towns; they were constantly intermarrying with the Gaelic houses, and also constantly at war, chiefly with the Ormonds. One small point will show how completely they had become Irish: Thomas Earl of Desmond had fought and captured Edmund Butler, and the ransom which he demanded consisted of two manuscripts, the *Book of Carrick* and the *Psalter of Cashel*. One even finds them, in the matter of dynastic succession, at times abandoning the feudal custom of immediate descent and adopting a form of selection of the most suitable, on the Irish model: in virtue of this, Earl Thomas was driven out and robbed of his inheritance by his uncle

James, who nevertheless obtained recognition (1413).
How could they fail to gravitate more and more outside
the English orbit? The King in London had other matters to occupy him, with the war in France and then the
War of the Roses. His best men, such as Sir John Talbot,
who was twice Lord Deputy, when in Ireland were only
thinking of how they could get to France, where both
glory and profit were to be earned. The climax was
reached when the Kildares became Lords Deputy.

Even the coming to the throne of the harsh Tudors
made no change. Henry VII, a Lancastrian, distrusted
Earl Gerald, who had supported the Yorkist cause; he
relieved him of his charge, which he had held since 1478,
and consigned him to the Tower, naming in his place a
pure Englishman, Sir Edward Poynings.[6] Nevertheless
after this display of energy, being aware that (apart from
an enormous military and financial effort, which he did
not dare to undertake) he would be unable to control
Ireland without the cooperation of the great Anglo-Norman houses, Henry issued the famous verdict: "Since all
Ireland cannot rule this Earl, let this Earl rule all Ireland!" Whether genuine or not, this saying described the
true state of affairs. Garrett Mór or Gerald the Great,
who was reinstalled as Lord Deputy in 1496, remained
in the office till his death in 1513. He had only just returned from the Tower when he sent his son in "fosterage" to the King of Tirconnell, Hugh O'Donnell the Red,
which was the closest link known in the Gaelic custom.
He also married three of his five daughters to Irish chief-

[6] He was the author of the famous Poynings Law of which we
shall hear more later: it renewed the statutes of Kilkenny, going
even further than they did, in that from then onwards it subordinated the Parliament of the Kingdom of Ireland to the King in
his Council, as well as to the Lord Deputy in his Privy Council
in Dublin (1495).

tains. During those fifteen years he was once again to
reign with no external control, much as an Ard Rí of the
old days.

Chapter 8.   The End of the Great Men of
              Ireland

The thunderbolt came twenty years later. Garrett Óg, or
Gerald the Younger, had succeeded his father and held
his office, with a few breaks till his death; but he met with
opposition such as Gerald the Great never experienced.
The Privy Council of Dublin, which was more and more
packed with purely English elements, notably John Allen, Archbishop and Chancellor, denounced him secretly;
Sir Piers Butler, who was his own brother-in-law, but a
Butler, also conspired against him; the all-powerful Cardinal Wolsey stirred up against him the jealousy of Henry
VIII by his mocking allusions to "King Kildare"; and
Sir Thomas Butler, who had become Earl of Ormond, still
used the favor of Anne Boleyn, a relation of the Butlers,
as a weapon against him. From 1520 till 1522 Kildare
was deprived of his office, and then restored. In 1534 he
was summoned to London and placed in the Tower; before leaving he had handed over his lieutenancy to his
son, a young man of twenty, who was known as Silken
Thomas because of the pride which he took in dressing
himself and his bodyguard in clothes of flashing satin.
Kildare's enemies, with diabolic skill, spread a rumor that
he had died in prison; Silken Thomas rushed to Dublin
in a rage, flung the sword of state on to the council
table, and solemnly announced his defiance of the Tudor
king. He was urged on to this rash rejoinder, it is said,

by the bantering song of his Irish harpist. In the tumult
which followed, Allen was killed and Thomas thereupon
excommunicated: Gerald died in prison of sorrow, in
December, as the result of this. In October Sir William
Skeffington had landed with a large force, and Ormond
rose in his support; Maynooth, which was the chief center of the rebellion, yielded in eight days, and the sur-
vivors were hanged: being overwhelmed on all sides,
Silken Thomas gave himself up. Five of his uncles, who
were taken in various traps, followed him to the scaffold
at Tyburn in 1537. Only a child of ten survived, one
Gerald, whom Henry made every effort to capture and
to destroy; he was saved by the conspiracy of the whole
of Ireland, and lived first at Florence and then in France,
where they thought of using him against Henry. He
ended by returning in humble fashion after eighteen
years, and submitted. . . . The Fitzgeralds of Kildare
were tamed for good and all.

[The truth is that their state of semi-royalty was an
anachronism, even in their time, and can only be accounted for by the reluctance of the Tudor kings to come
to blows. The introduction of firearms, musket, and especially of cannon had completely altered the balance of
power between the Crown and the great families. No
castle could now hold out against artillery. Besides, the
authoritarian monarchies were coming into being which
were to lead in the national conflicts of the sixteenth
century] James I hanged The MacDonnell, King of the
Isles, in 1499, and Francis I struck down the High Constable of France—these were the Scottish and French
equivalents of the ruin of the Kildares. The great families
of Ireland were so fully aware of this, and of how it was
impossible for them to resist on their own in the future,
that they inaugurated the policy which was to be instinc-

tive of Ireland in the following centuries, that of counter-
balancing their weakness by means of foreign alliances.
One thus finds James, the eleventh Earl of Desmond,
between the years 1523 and 1529, summoning Francis
I and Charles V to his aid, and in 1549 O'Neill and
O'Donnell offering their homage to Henry II of France in
consideration of an expedition which set out from Brest
to their assistance, and was only thwarted by a storm;
finally, when Edward VI was obviously soon to die,
Noailles, the French ambassador, proposed the support
of France for Lady Jane Grey, in return for the cession
of Ireland.

Meanwhile, the Reformation followed its course. Henry
VIII imposed on Ireland the Act of Supremacy, which
made him the head of the Church of England, and in
order to do this assumed the new title of King of Ireland in 1541; only thus was ended the fiction, which up
to then had been uncontested, that the Pope was the
true sovereign lord of the island, the king being only
his deputy by procuration. The innovations of Henry
VIII, which still preserved the essentials of the Faith,
while they were not much liked in Ireland, nevertheless
made no great stir, for the ordinary man was still able
to go to Mass. What did cause consternation, however,
was the destruction of the beautiful abbeys, Dunbrody,
Tintern, and Baltinglass, which for centuries had been
objects of veneration and which were now, by a stroke
of the pen, destroyed, despoiled, and dismembered. In
Dublin great sorrow was caused when the populace saw
Browne the Archbishop publicly burning the *bachall
Iosa* (the *baculum Jesu*), which our Lord had come down
from heaven to present to St. Patrick. The opposition
which broke out when the *Book of Common Prayer* was
introduced under Edward VI proved that there was only

a handful of true Protestants in the country; but it was not till later, from 1560 onwards, under Elizabeth, who was personally indifferent, that persecution really raged, when, for instance, Dermot O'Hurley, the Archbishop of Cashel, was put to death after horrible tortures.

The independence of the great families, whether feudal or Gaelic, was now being fought for at the far ends of the island, in Desmond and in Ulster. On the death of Conn Bacach O'Neill, the King of Tyrone, in 1548, the Castle supported his eldest son, Matthew, though he was said to be illegitimate, against another son, Shane, who, however, ousted him and because of his haughtiness became known as "Shane the Proud." He was acknowledged as The O'Neill, with the full ancient Gaelic ceremonial, on the sacred stone. He declared: "My ancestors were Kings of Ulster—Ulster is mine and mine it shall remain." Matthew having been killed in a skirmish, his young son Hugh—whom we shall meet again—was taken to London, to be brought up in the house of the Earl of Leicester. As for Shane, he started writing to Elizabeth letters in Latin which were both sweet and flattering; he even had the audacity to pay her a visit, surrounded by his tall gallow-glasses, and returned home not only with his head on his shoulders but apparently in high favor. Neither of these two comedians, however, was deceived by the other. In 1561 Lord Deputy Sussex wished to attack him, and later Sidney, but both in vain. An attempt was made to poison him. Shane was nevertheless able to make sure of his domination over the whole of Ulster; in the East he overcame the MacDonnells of Antrim, whom he conquered at Glenshesk, and in the West the O'Donnells, whose chieftain he took prisoner. He returned against them in the following year, but with the energy of despair they routed him, this time at Farsetmore.

Whether his mind was unbalanced by this, or whether he relied simply on their chivalry, he decided to seek shelter with his former victims, the MacDonnells; the latter, who were true Scotsmen, gave him a great welcome; but a quarrel on a point of honor broke out after they had been drinking, and Shane O'Neill was stabbed to death. His head, which was sold to Dublin, was placed to rot on the battlements of the Castle. Thus did this meteor of Irish independence pass away in 1567, at the age of thirty-five.

Then came the turn of the other Fitzgeralds, those of Desmond. It was not that the Earl had any wish to fight; but he was a marked man, for he lived too far off, he was too great and too free, and his palatinate gave cause for uneasiness. Furthermore, young gentlemen had begun to appear, the Carews, the Raleighs, and the Grenvilles, who were on the make and intended to amass large fortunes rapidly in the "colony." Finally, the house of Ormond, which was on the side of the Crown, wished to make an end of the rival house, which had the reputation of not being so at all. In 1565 Earl Thomas fought and captured Earl Gerald, who remained a prisoner in London till 1573; his relation, Fitzmaurice, kept up the struggle till he was eventually overcome and had to fly to the continent. The religious persecution in the country, which was growing harsher, the cleavage of Europe between Protestants and Catholics, now gave the Gaelic resistance a confessional note, which provided a new element. Appeals were made to Philip II and to the Pope. Fitzmaurice, who returned in 1579, soon perished in a skirmish. A small force of Spaniards, only about eight hundred in number, landed in 1580 at Smerwick in Kerry, but had to yield when confronted with cannon, and were put to the sword. Earl Gerald himself, being driven into a corner, came out openly as a rebel, and though beaten and surrounded, held his own for three years; it was difficult to capture him in those Munster forests, protected as he was by a general conspiracy. Then Sir John Perrot, a bastard of Henry VIII, who was President of Munster, set to work and scientifically devastated the country, burning the harvest and massacring the herds, which were the only source of livelihood of this pastoral people, and deliberately produced a famine. Gerald was finally sold, surprised, and killed. Out of the 2,000,000 hectares which were thus released, seigniories were carved out for the "undertakers," that is to say, those who had undertaken the fresh conquest. Of these, Raleigh received 16,-000, and the poet Spenser, the author of the *Faerie Queen,* also received a vast demesne. The day of the Fitzgeralds of the South was over.

However, in the North, Ulster was still intact. Hugh O'Neill had with prudence slowly made himself master. He started by modestly becoming Lord Dungannon, after his father, Matthew, then became Earl of Tyrone, as an English title, then O'Neill according to the ancient Gaelic title, and all the time gave the appearance of being on the side of the Crown; the English found in him a new and enigmatic type of adversary. He had spent some years in London, close to the court. He understood modern conditions, both English and European; this chieftain of a clan was a politician of the international order; he was fifty years old and knew how to play his game. Beside him, Hugh O'Donnell the Red, twenty-five years old and a soul of fire, understood the older man; there was no hope of survival except by the sword, and the fact had to be faced; it was necessary to unite instead of fighting each other, and to build up a national spirit; Hugh would serve under O'Neill. At the age of fifteen he had been treacherously seized and taken to the Castle, where he was held as a prisoner for four years; he had escaped, and his feet had been frozen in the mountain snows. He had no love for the English.⌉

The struggle, which had been smoldering since 1573, suddenly burst into flame, and for ten years, from 1594 to 1603, though there were periods of quiet, there were also periods of violence. O'Neill, well entrenched in his inaccessible stronghold of Ulster, temporized, for he was calculating and setting his hopes on James VI of Scotland, on Philip of Spain, and especially on the death of Elizabeth. In spite of his victories at Clontibret and at the Yellow Ford, and his regular troops who were at last armed with the musket, he had no illusions as to his fundamental weakness or the great resources of England: he tried to overcome London with weariness, boredom, and disgust. For a short period his glory unified Ireland, where he was able to move freely from North to South. He wore out Essex, who bore down on him with an army of sixteen thousand men, then hesitated and concluded a truce, for which on his return he paid with his head. In 1600 Mountjoy landed with an army of twenty thousand soldiers, complete with modern equipment, and adopted Perrot's cruel idea of destroying the people by hunger. The Munster rising was repressed with such savagery that "scarcely a cow could be heard lowing from Dunquin in Kerry to Cashel in Munster" (*Pacata Hibernia*). Niall Garbh O'Donnell, a relative of Red Hugh, had been bought over by the Castle, and rose now against him and O'Neill. The Spaniards arrived at last but they were a disappointment, for they only numbered four thousand men and had an irresolute leader in del Aguila, who, instead of moving on to Ulster, shut himself up in the little southern port of Kinsale, where Mountjoy immediately

besieged him. No matter! By forced marches, sometimes up to forty miles a day, the kings of the North
swept down and laid siege to the besieger. It was enough
now to wait, for Mountjoy, as was always the case in
adverse circumstances, was rapidly melting down. At the
request of del Aguila and in answer to the entreaties of
Red Hugh, O'Neill attacked, though against his own better judgment; liaison was not properly achieved, and one
day's disaster ruined the work of ten years. O'Donnell
made for Spain in order to seek for help; there he died,
probably poisoned by James Blake, an agent employed
by London. O'Neill submitted and lived for a few more
years an impoverished, humiliated, and uneasy life in his
native Tyrone, after which, feeling that his life was in
danger, he set sail and went to die in Rome, where his
grave can be seen in the little Church of San Pietro in
Montorio. Beneath the tombstone there lay with him another dead, the Gaelic Ireland of the ancient days (1616).

Chapter 9. The Structure of Gaelic Society

It took five centuries to destroy this Gaelic society, though
it was assailed by overpowering forces, Roman, Scandinavian, Norman, and English—if indeed it has ever been
destroyed and does not still survive, though obscurely, in
certain modern tendencies of the Irish outlook; it must
have had a tremendous hold on its own people, to have
been able to go on showing such powers of recovery and
absorption. We know it almost in detail, but these very
details, and especially the legal texts, are very difficult to
grasp, just because they are so original. But the docu-
ments still exist; we have, for instance, in regard to the

political structure, that *Book of Rights* which was compiled by Cormac Mac Cuilennain, the King-Bishop of Cashel, about the year 903, and which was corrected later at the orders of Brian Boru in his own interest; this consists of a series of didactic poems, setting out for each of the seven states which were then in existence its rights and its duties, the tributes and the gifts which it had the right to levy or was bound to offer.

The social unit in this society was the *fine,* or the family, by which we must not understand the more limited family of modern times but the ancient Indo-European *gens*. When complete and perfect (*deirbhfine*) it extended for four generations, from the father (the *cenn fine* or head of the *gens*) to his great-grandson; thence it swarmed in branches which were held to be different, and as the result of the swarming there was a division of estate, the gavelkind, which seems so astonishing to the outside observer; as a natural consequence of this, the right of succession ceased in the royal houses.[7] A special feature of the Gaelic family was the custom of fosterage; the child, till it was seventeen years old, was trusted to the care of some house with which the family was on friendly terms; this interchange produced a link between it and its foster parents which was as strong as, it not stronger than, that which existed between it and its parents by blood. Fosterage was as potent as the Roman adoption, but it was not so circumscribed legally; it went as deep but was wider in scope, had also its emotional and moral aspect. When considering the tenacity of the institution one should remember that even Daniel O'Connell, at the end of the

[7] The word clann (children) which is so often inaccurately used by historians, has no precise legal content; it merely indicates descent from a common ancestor.

eighteenth century, was thus transferred by adoption to a family.

The basic political unit was the *tuath* (= people, or tribe): it was a unit because it was self-sufficient, both in its elementary economy and also in its organization. It had its king, a kind of patriarch, who united all powers in himself, being leader in war, diplomat, and judge; it had its social hierarchy, which was very exactly defined, whether according to class, with nobles, freemen, and slaves, or according to functions, with ecclesiastics, men of letters, and lawyers. And, as one would expect in an essentially rural community, dignities were connected with the possession of land, of cattle, and of horses, and with a certain household. Even the kinds of foods and the coloring of clothes are prescribed by the ancient texts in order to distinguish the various ranks. An original office, but one which was considered essential, was that of the hospitaler, who had to keep open house for all comers and who, in order to meet his heavy expense, had the right to 800 hectares of land and to a host of servants; he held the rank of a local king, as did the bishop and the man of letters. At the foot of the ladder, of which each step was exactly determined, with nobles, minor nobles, players on the harp, tradesmen, vassals, hired valets, there was the humble male or female slave, the *mug* or *cumal*, who, in primitive times, before the introduction of money, represented a standard of value. In this strictly aristocratic structure, each member had a different weight, according to his riches and his rank; and these various weights defined for each member the "honor price," with its attendant privileges. The "honor price" carried with it the "price of blood," as it is clear that in the case of a murder, it would cost more for a man of importance, less for a man of none. For, of course, as is always the case in primitive communities, expiation might take the form of an indemnity.

Two classes were specially noticeable in this Gaelic community. One was that of the *brehons,* professional men who were entrusted with the work of drawing up the laws, and also of defining the meaning of the law at the court of the prince. They brought talmudic subtlety to bear on their science, as when they laid down that if a wound received from behind disqualified a king, this did not apply to any wound which reached through from front to back! Punishments were harsh, and included outlawing, blinding, death by drowning and beheading. These *brehons* received great honor, both in the reverence paid to them and in actual wealth; and their system of law, no doubt because it was so well adapted to ordinary needs, was one of the social structures that English law had most difficulty in breaking down.

Another class was the hereditary one of men of letters, which was perhaps even more important. As in earlier days the druids were succeeded by the *filidh,* so now, by an imperceptible evolution to which it is difficult to ascribe a date, the *filidh* were succeeded by the bards. The bard was at the same time troubadour and minstrel. Being attached to a princely house, who maintained him in the height of opulence and honor, he sang of the glories of his masters, their battles, their alliances and their genealogies, and by reason of this he was already becoming a keeper of the annals and an antiquary. In fact, besides being a poet, he was both scholar and archivist. Being a technician in his art, he was also grammarian, philologist, and an expert in prosody. Besides, as he was armed with his verse, round which there always floated a dreaded *aura,* in the old days that of magic, later that of satire, he continued to wield a moral power, all the more to be feared in that it was immaterial, one of inspiration and of censure, capable of restraining or of unloosing princes, and one which with good reason the English were to try and destroy, though for a long time without success: "to cease providing for the bards," is an article that one constantly finds them inserting into treaties. They sometimes tried to use this elusive influence for their own benefit; Mountjoy seduced Angus O'Daly with money to write poems against the Gaelic chieftains, a satire which was so bitterly resented that a faithful Irishman killed the mocking traitor. This corporation of the bards was so completely the soul of the Gaelic tradition that even after the collapse of the old indigenous order, when there were no longer any great houses to keep it alive and to support it, and though it was languishing and feeble; yet it did not die out for at least two centuries. The difference is that it came down from the castles to the farmhouses and the highways. The wandering poets of the eighteenth century were the last heirs of the bards, as perhaps were also the "hedge schoolmasters," i.e., the masters who, in defiance of the English law, held schools under the shelter of the hedges. So true was it that for centuries the bards had been that essential part of society —opinion.

Gaelic society, however, which was so closely and so firmly woven together in the smaller groups, was unsuccessful in its attempt to organize itself on the higher levels. Was it precisely because of this closely woven fabric that it considered that there was no need for the state? There certainly were, above the local kings, the higher kings, those of the seven kingdoms, but it was understood that they would only intervene in quarrels between their vassals, who continued to be masters in their own territory. Above all, the High King only carried any weight by chance, if he had the personal strength to do so. This is proved by the fact that, after Brian Boru, for a hundred and fifty years there were only High Kings "with opposition," which is equivalent to saying that there were no High Kings at all. Another proof is that the first act of a High King—if he was able to do so—was to tour Ireland "on circuit," in order to collect tribute and hostages, the pledge of an obedience on which it is clear that, short of these precautions, he could not count. The country's attempts at organizing its unity never succeeded.

Another cause of weakness was the custom governing succession in the great houses. This was by election among a limited number of candidates. Every member of the royal *deirbh-fine* was eligible, and this naturally led to rivalry. But every member who was outside the *deirbh-fine,* that is to say, whose family had had no reigning king for three generations, ceased to be eligible, and this brought about cabals among those who were threatened by this limiting condition. In the Middle Ages the Gaelic dynasties, which had been impressed by the stability of the feudal lineages but were repelled by the automatic quality of primogeniture, tried to make their position more sure, and this led to the institution of the *tanaiste rig* or deputy king who was the heir presumptive; habit, however, proved too strong, and when the king died rivalries sprang up and led to civil war.

And, again, this society was unable for too long a time to organize itself for defense. It held fast to an epic conception of war. The chieftain led his men into battle at the time when they could be spared from work in the fields; each one did his best, and that was all; there was scarcely a shadow of armament, of organization, or tactics; they relied purely on natural valor. *The War of the Gael and the Gall* (an eleventh century manuscript

translated by Dr. James H. Todd in 1867) tells the tale of
the battle of Clontarf as if it were part of the Iliad, consisting of a series of single combats. Now, Norman chivalry
had little that was chivalrous about it; it was a machine as
carefully thought out as the technique of the age allowed.
The Gaelic levies, which were frequently far more numerous, were unable to hold out against English armies of
the sixteenth century, which, though usually small, had
the most modern equipment. They did not start wearing
chain mail till the fourteenth century. Even in 1514, at
the battle of Cnoc Tuagh, they were still arrayed as in the
Middle Ages, with bows and crossbows. As they gradually
became aware of their military inferiority, they reinforced
themselves with professional soldiers, the *bonaght,* who
were Irish, and especially the *galloglaigh* (in English
gallowglasses), recruited in the Hebrides and in Scotland who, with their tall stature, their axes, their coats of
mail, and their intrepid courage—840 out of 900 fell on
the battlefield at Kinsale—held out for a long time, even
in the face of muskets.[8] Hugh O'Neill was the first Gaelic
chieftain to try and build up a modern force; but he
had no foundries or workshops of his own and had to
import everything from Glasgow, and, without any artillery worth speaking of, he was powerless against the
towns.

In spite of all these weaknesses and archaisms—perhaps because of them—this Gaelic society must have
exercised an immense attraction, since for centuries it

---

[8] For a long time the mercenaries received no pay in the strict
sense of the word; their master quartered them on the inhabitants,
at whose expense they lived. It is easy to imagine that such a
system was liable to abuse. This was the right of "coyne and
livery," which provided the chieftain with hired troops at a small
cost, and which the English Government was for the same
reason constantly trying to forbid.

was able to assimilate its conquerors, the Danes, the Normans, and even the English. And it was really not surprising that feudal lords and aristocrats were able to take their place without friction in a society which itself was so aristocratic in spirit. The pride of race, which was so strong in those indigenous houses which went back to the Flood, touched them in their most intimate spot; they ended by sharing in it and it became part of themselves. For in those ancient times, if an innate sense of superiority was to be found, it was on the Gaelic side. When Lord Deputy Sidney made a tour of Connacht in 1575, he noticed with surprise that the Prendergasts had taken the name of MacMorris, the Nangles that of Costello, and that very few of them understood English. Even the descendants of the great du Bourg now called themselves MacWilliam; and once upon a time they were to be seen, on their return from Dublin, as soon as they were past the Shannon and in their own country, making a gesture of defiance in face of the citadel of Athlone, as they contemptuously threw off the legal English dress and proudly assumed the Gaelic mantle.

II. THE DEATH STRUGGLE OF GAELIC IRELAND

Chapter 10. The Policy of the Plantations

After Kinsale an act of amnesty was granted by James I (James VI of Scotland), who succeeded Elizabeth. He was the son of Mary Stuart, and there were those who persisted in their illusion that he was a Catholic at heart; Ireland set great hopes in him. He was actually an unpleasing pedant obsessed with theology, a fanatic for his divine rights, and, no doubt, even in matters of conscience, claimed obedience in the name of the famous *Cujus regio ejus religio* (whose the region, his the religion). That is why Mountjoy soon came in person to reduce the southern ports by force, which had been notoriously faithful during the struggle, but which had claimed the right, in virtue of their liberties, to restore the Mass in public. Now not only were the Catholics in an overwhelming majority but, furthermore, the Church "by law established" showed no zeal for their conversion. Spenser himself deplored the contrast between the apathy of the Protestant ministers, "fat and idle in their well-warmed nests," and the zeal of the priests coming from Spain or from Rome, who had no

56

hopes for gain in this world and were risking their lives in order to keep their flock loyal to the ancient faith. The Anglican Bishop Bedell was a *rara avis* who at least set out to provide a Gaelic Bible, the only one to appear during two centuries; it looked as if the Protestant clergy preferred to see the indigenous population remaining Papist and thus excluded from the protection of the law. This law, which was a menace forever hanging over their heads, was at times allowed to fall into abeyance, whilst at others, as in the days of Lord Deputy Chichester (1604-1616), it was rigorously applied, with the fines for "recusancy" pouring in (that is, for refusing to take the Oath of Supremacy), as decreed by the Court of High Commission.

The reason was that, *pari passu*, the policy of "plantations" was in full swing. The idea, which was a hateful one, was nothing new: interestingly enough, it was first put into operation under Mary Tudor, the Catholic Queen: Leix and Offaly, which had become the counties of the Queen and the King (Philip of Spain), had been emptied of those who had a lawful right to the land, the O'Mores and the O'Connors, and made over to colonists of English origin, who were "planted" on condition that they only imported and employed English labor; the aim was to replace a less reliable population by one on which the government could count. Later on, there was the further aim of replacing a Catholic by a Protestant population; in proportion as the Reformation went ahead in England and as she became the chief rampart facing the Roman counteroffensive, even so did religious become mixed up with political motives; both of these, it will be understood, spurred on by the cupidity of the invaders, whose only aim was to make large and rapid fortunes at the expense of the conquered people.

The procedure was as follows: the lawyers, such as Sir John Davies, who was Attorney-General under Chichester, would bring a charge of disloyalty against some individual, whose case would then be brought before a jury assembled for the purpose; the bill of accusation, or indictment, once it had been passed, was sent on to the King's Bench, which pronounced that the lands of the accused were forfeit to the Crown, in virtue of attainder; it only remained for Parliament to ratify this, and it had the force of law. There were always ways of intimidating the jury, such as leaving it for three days without food or drink, or else imposing on it vast fines, as much as £4,000 a head, if it should venture to vote the wrong way. It was under such conditions that one Richard Boyle, the son of a lowly man, was able to arrive from London with £27 in his pocket and to die loaded with wealth, Earl of Cork, a peer of Ireland, with his four sons peers like himself, and himself in receipt of an income, so it was said, of £50 a day. Ireland herself was so reduced by this policy that on the one hand she could only rebel, though without hope, since submission could not assure her of the elementary rights of religion and bread; from this were revived those wars to the finish, as when the O'Mores fought for fifty years to defend their lands, and only yielded when they were exterminated; even during the periods of drowsiness when she seemed at last to be resigned, Ireland was merely meditating on how she would avenge herself in the end. On the other hand, as persecution and confiscation went hand in hand, so did national and religious sentiments draw so close to each other that they eventually became confused together, and the Catholic clergy came to take a leading part in politics which they have never lost: the Irish people could no longer distinguish between the defense of their lives and the defense of their faith.

The "plantation" of Munster after 1583—which was at least an act of war intended to wipe out forever the memory of the Fitzgeralds—came to nothing; later risings and the sale and resale of titles to land left the remains of the ancient peasantry at the end of a few years where they were before. That of Ulster was another matter, for it was done in a time of peace and in cold blood. A Gaelic chieftain, Sir Cahir O'Doherty, who up to then had been on good terms with the government, quarreled with Paulet, the Governor of Derry. Paulet hit him. O'Doherty captured and burnt Derry, killed Paulet, and soon afterwards also perished. Thereupon, the machine was started off, 500,000 acres were confiscated and portioned out, of which only 50,000 went back to the original inhabitants. The "undertakers," who received from 1000 to 2000 acres per head, were only to give leases to Scottish and English farmers, who, as can be imagined, would sublet to the small Irish farmers, but with no title and therefore revocable *ad nutum*. Many of the immigrants came from Yorkshire, and even more from Scotland, and were specially favored by King James, who had strong clannish instincts. Derry had been conceded to a group of speculators in London, who had advanced money; from that time onwards it was known as Londonderry. Many of the newcomers were Presbyterians who had been persecuted in their own country by the Established Church, and these increased in number as the persecution became more acute. Thus came into being the peculiar new Ulster (1601-1611), a citadel of Protestantism, but with half the Protestants dissenters, in which there lived side by side, in a state of mutual hatred, with rancor on one side and defiance on the other, two peoples who were foreign to each other—those who had been despoiled living in the unfertile mountains which alone had been left to them, while the spoiler lived in the rich lowlands. There was here a train of powder only waiting to catch fire.

Nevertheless, everything still remained in a state of suspense. On the one hand, the Catholics were constantly playing the card of "loyalty," and the attainder of the great O'Neill was voted in Parliament without there being any resistance; they claimed that the Statutes of Kilkenny were out of date, and all the subjects of the kingdom were equal without distinction before the common law. And yet this same so-called common law, if applied, forbade Catholics to practice at the bar, to open a school, or to take a university degree in that College of Trinity which had been recently founded by Elizabeth as a center of English and Protestant influence. The great men of the Anglo-Norman nobility, when they went to King James with the petition that their religion should no longer exclude them from his service, that is, from public duties, met with a rebuff for being Papist. Their Church, he declared, in that peculiar manner of his, half bantering and half pedantic at the same time, authorized regicide; and yet at the same time he raised some of them to peerages, even the descendants of the old Gaelic kings; for MacDonnell was made Lord Antrim. O'Brien at the same time was made Lord Inchiquin. Meanwhile Ussher, the Anglican Archbishop of Armagh and Provost of the University, was declaring that "the religion of the Papists is superstitious and heretical" and "to tolerate it is a grave sin. . . . Everything was still in a state of suspense.

The accession of Charles I brought fresh disillusionment for the oppressed. His wife, Henrietta of France, who was an ardent Catholic, gave rise to vain hopes. With his favorite, Thomas Wentworth, who became Lord Deputy in 1632 and was made Lord Strafford in 1639, a new element, and one foreign to Ireland, entered into the game, that of the struggle between the royal "prerogative" and the authority of Parliament. Strafford (the great red ruins of his castle can still be seen on the Naas road) was, like his friend, Laud, the Archbishop of Canterbury, influenced by two ideas: to impose the absolute power of the prince and in all things to forge right through, to be *thorough*. He was an excellent and courageous administrator, but he could act the tyrant on behalf of what he believed to be just, tyranny included; he thus contemplated a "plantation" of Connacht, which he did not have time to bring about. He had a far greater distrust of the Protestants who were in possession, and were therefore dangerous, than of the despoiled Gaels, who were obedient and whose very religion, as he knew, made them look with favor on royalism. What he was trying to bring about was that Ireland should not be a source of expense to the King but of revenue and of strength to help him curb the Parliament in London; in 1639 he was able to offer Charles a subsidy of £200,000, payable in three years, and a well-equipped, well-officered army of 9000 men, under the command of the Earl of Ormond, a Protestant but a staunch royalist. The recall of Strafford in November 1639 and his execution in May 1641 brought these plans to nothing. The scene was set for a fresh tragedy, the saddest of all, which was to last for twelve years.

Chapter 11.   The Confederation of Kilkenny

This tragedy began in October 1641, with an unsuccessful attempt to take Dublin Castle by surprise, and simultaneously with a peasants' revolt in Ulster. Peasants and Gaelic chieftains such as Sir Phelim O'Neill, who had been hunted down thirty years ago, now started hunting their hunters and massacred a considerable number of them, perhaps as many as 10,000. In London it was claimed that the number was 200,000 and England, horrified, worse still, being challenged, saw red; hence the pitiless nature of this war. It should be remarked that when these "Sicilian Vespers" broke out the King and the London Parliament had not yet come to open warfare, and the affair could thus be legally regarded as a rebellion. But instead of entering into the endless detail of marches and countermarches, of combats, secret negotiations and underhand dealings, it is better to try and disentangle the interests which were involved, interests of infinite complexity, due to the complexity, at the time, of the Irish social structure, but also due to the other interests which had found their way in and were making the situation more warped, and which were apart from those of the nation, some of them English and some European.

First of all, the old historic nation was fighting to recover or to keep the land; by the nation we must now understand the mixture, no longer merely of the original Gaels and the Danes but also of the Anglo-Normans and of those English of the Pale who had remained Catholic, all threatened equally by the greed of the "undertakers," and from then onwards all considered as a more or less helot race, subject to eviction at the will of the "planted" colonist. Even a very great lord like Ormond, who was both a Protestant and a loyalist, wondered whether he was not in danger of coming under the same fate, and at the end of the war both he and Inchiquin were attainted. There were those who had been despoiled, such as Rory O'More, and those who were threatened with this fate. There were those who dreamt of a complete restitution, even of a return of the ancient Gaelic order, and those who took a more modest view and merely wished to bring the confiscations to an end, and those who, even more humble, only hoped to beg for a few favors for themselves.

And the same tendencies began to show themselves in religious matters. For the two things were inextricably mingled. It was just the fact that they were Catholics which exposed the diverse members of the ancient society to spoliation; and the common danger welded them together in the defense of their faith. There again, one can distinguish a thousand nuances, ranging from extreme prudence to extreme intransigence, not only in the characters involved but also in the points of view and the various vocations. Faithful as were the laity, it was the clergy, whose lives were so completely centered on doctrine, who proved themselves specially intractable; the Jesuits, for instance, who ran the risk of death and martyrdom for the cause, and the Nuncio, who had come directly from Rome for the defense of the faith. Finally, the indissoluble alloy in which the defense of the nation and the defense of religion had been cast could not fail to plunge the clergy into politics; the ascendancy of the clergy, and the use of spiritual weapons in the struggle, became more and more noticeable; one even finds two prelates, Queely of Tuam and MacMahon of Clogher,

leading their men into battle, one of whom ended by being killed and the other by being hanged.

These were the specifically Irish influences which were
at work, but there was one notion which was not Irish
and which was producing cleavages of a very different
kind: which side should be supported in the struggle
between the Crown and Parliament? It was clear (and
the King was aware of this) that Ireland, being Catholic,
was monarchical in sentiment; and the King was tempted
to make use of Ireland in order to curb the power of
Parliament, though he also felt considerable apprehen-
sion in regard to this, for he knew how much indignation
such a move would cause in England; his interests thus
presented him with two alternatives; Ireland, it is scarcely
necessary to say, lost in both. There were, furthermore,
other elements besides those who were Catholic by tradition: Ormond, who was a Protestant, was a royalist and
very staunch, owing to feudal fidelity, a sense of mutual
interest, and patriotism as well; the same might perhaps
be said of Inchiquin, though in his case he came of the
most ancient Gaelic lineage. And there were others, such
as Lord Broghill, a son of the Earl of Cork, who started
by being royalists and then passed over to the other side
—in order to save their goods.

On top of that, external ideas and forces were bearing
on the Irish tragedy and would cause things to get even
worse: there were the forces let loose by the English civil
war, once it had broken out; there were also the policies
of the great Continental monarchies, not as yet that of
Spain, which was holding aloof, but rather that of France,
with Richelieu and Mazarin, and especially that of the
Holy See, the influence of which was brought to bear, as
indeed it should be, on the point of contact where the
Reformation and the Counter-Reformation were con-

fronting each other, and which was coming to the rescue. It was clear that, if a choice had to be made, Rome, as was its duty, would set the cause of religion before that of the country.

One final circumstance is to be considered: there was a class of noblemen in the country, both Gaelic and Anglo-Norman, whose only calling, from time immemorial, had been that of the sword. As they were excluded from the King's service because of the fact that they were Catholics, Strafford had not hesitated to pack them into the army which he was building up for the royal cause. After his death, when this army had been disbanded, thousands of soldiers and hundreds of officers were wandering about who were past masters at their trade and were only seeking for employment for their swords. If only supplies could be sent to Ireland, she would be swarming with men ready for war.

In reply to the events in Ulster, London passed the "Adventurers' Act" in 1642. The "Adventurers" were the speculators who, with the prospect of future confiscations, subscribed, that is "adventured," money for the waging of war. An essential clause of the law naturally forbade in advance any clemency for the rebels: otherwise, what guarantee would the investors have had? A little later, Ormond, who had been made a marquis, was nominated as Lord Lieutenant and rallied round him the English elements who continued to be royalists. In August the Dublin Parliament met, but this time, through the efforts of the Lords-Justice, Parsons and Borlase had been purged of all Catholics. Those who had been expelled formed the Confederation of Kilkenny in October, which was the embryo of the provisional government; this gave the insurrection a kind of legitimacy and order. Their aim was not at all to repudiate the Crown but the more modest one of obtaining the restitution of lands which had been confiscated for religious reasons, liberty of conscience and equality of status for Catholics, and finally the repeal of the Poynings Law, which kept the Irish assemblies in a state of impotence. In Kilkenny, a town belonging to Ormond, the Confederation remained under his influence; Ormond continued to act as mediator between it and the King in the negotiations which were constantly taking place, though the war was now in full swing. The Council, being new to the work, was afflicted with a lack of cohesion and obsessed with the idea of setting up a governmental machine instead of waging war; its efforts became diluted through having four armies divided between the four provinces, and the clerical element rejected on principle all efforts to make a peace unsatisfactory to the Church while at the same time it was incompetent to provide the weapons for waging war.

A great soldier had, however, arisen, Owen Roe O'Neill, (*i.e.,* the Red). He was the nephew of the great Hugh, and had been at Kinsale when he was fifteen years old; he had distinguished himself in the service of Spain with his fine defense of Arras against the French. He was a soldier in the modern style, who wished to have an army, no matter how small, provided it should be paid, fed, equipped, and disciplined, and whose officers, if recalcitrant, should be offered the choice of obedience or execution. He was also a statesman in the modern style, who wished for a united Ireland, no longer consisting of clans or provinces, the orders of whose government he, as a soldier, would be the first to obey, while he rejected with a smile the accusation that he wished to become King. His victory at Benburb, in 1646, was nullified by the incapacity of the Council. Charles, who had been weakened by his defeat at Naseby in 1645, offered terms which, though they were not brilliant, were anyway acceptable; they were known as "the Peace of Ormond." It was urgent either to accept them or to march on Dublin: neither was done. Rinuccini, the Nuncio, who had landed with money and arms and who was therefore in a position to call the tune, insisted on a fight to the finish, even under threat of excommunication. Meanwhile, Ormond lost hope and "if he had to choose between rebels, at least preferred English to Irish," and delivered Dublin to the Parliamentarians. The King was put to death and Ormond, who had returned, tried to recapture Dublin for Charles II, but in vain.

Everything was in a state of extreme confusion. Even the clergy were divided, and Rinuccini, being no longer obeyed, reembarked at Galway in February 1649. Owen Roe was dying, and then was dead.

With Dublin in the hands of the Parliamentarians, Ireland lay open to Cromwell who, with 20,000 men well supplied with artillery, took Drogheda in September 1649 where everyone was slaughtered in vengeance for those who had been killed in 1641 and as an example for the other garrisons; Wexford was treated in the same way; after a minor reverse at Clonmel, he left the completion of the work to his son-in-law, Ireton, who received the last capitulation, that of Galway, in 1652. There were at least 30,000 soldiers wandering about the country in bands, who could never be persuaded to give themselves up.[9] Efforts were made to get them off the stage, and thus

[9] There were for a long time, perhaps for half a century, small bands of irreconcilables who claimed that they lived by raids on the usurpers, and for that reason were looked on with a certain favor by the peasants, but who were gradually becoming semi-bandits. These minor Robin Hoods were known as "Tories" (a word which has lived on in the English political vocabulary) or "Rapparees."

began that flight of the "Wild Geese," who for a century
and a half were to swoop down under all the colors of
Europe—Spain, France, Austria, even Russia.

And now the fate of this Ireland, soaked in blood,
reduced to perhaps less than a million souls, and lying at
the feet of her conquerors, must be settled. To the puri-
tan spirit, nourished as it was on the savage stories of the
Old Testament, a few points were obvious in advance.
The chosen people must be avenged who had been deci-
mated by these Amalekites. Their capacity for revolt
must be broken once and for all, by removing from them
those powers which possession of the soil always renews.
It was also necessary to settle with the "adventurers" and,
another debt which was overdue, to pay the army, both
officers and men, who had received nothing for months.
That is why, as the confiscation which was at first contemplated, of 2,500,000 acres, was found to be too small,
it was decided to clear 11,000,000 (out of a general total
of 20,000,000) in order to satisfy all creditors, whether
men of the sword or men of the purse. Three quarters of
Ireland was handed over to them, only the last quarter,
Connacht and Clare, being reserved for the original inhabitants; those who had nothing but their hands to work
with were allowed to stay where they were, as they would
be useful as "hewers of wood and drawers of water," but
those who had possessed the land were deported in a body
"to hell or to Connacht," and they were left there to find
what compensation they could, at the expense of their
own people.

Cromwell, who died in September 1658, did not live
to see the reverse, anyway a partial one, which this fantastic enterprise met. As always happens, many of the soldiers sold their share, returned to their own homes, and
were seen no more. But there were also numbers of

speculators, even officers, who, having received the confiscated demesnes as their payment, settled there and
started a new class of proprietors alongside the old ones,
that of the Cromwellians. The ownership of the soil
was now completely changed. Before this transaction,
two thirds of it was still in Catholic hands; afterwards,
certainly no more than one third. The Protestants had also
taken the chief places in the towns and were dominant
in industry, in commerce, and in the liberal professions.
A deep cleavage was established everywhere on religious
lines. Ireland was beginning to assume her more modern
features and appearance.

Chapter 12. The Battle of the Boyne

The accession of Charles II in 1660 was received with
joy in Ireland. It was known that he had a secret weakness for the ancient religion (in which he insisted upon
dying), that he was humane and no fanatic. But he was
also a cynic, at least an opportunist, a kind of Louis
XVIII before his time, who was determined above all
things to keep his job; he remembered what his evenings
had been like at the Louvre under Mazarin, without
food or fire; and, being a prudent man, "he preferred
to sacrifice his friends rather than his enemies" (Curtis).
Besides, though the royal prerogative was far from being
extinct, it was henceforward balanced by Parliament;
and neither Parliament nor those whom Cromwell had
placed in possession in Ireland would have tolerated
a reversal of the new state of affairs. In vain did the
Catholics invoke the "Peace of Ormond," which had

been signed by Charles I in 1649 and which pledged the honor of his son. There thus were some special restitutions by royal favor, such as those to Lords Antrim and Inchiquin, but in general the "Act of Settlement" never set out to restore to the despoiled Catholics more than one third of their lands; and, indeed, after a few years no further claims were permitted; is there any example of a dispossessed class having ever regained its possessions? According to Sir William Petty, to whom we owe the famous *Down Survey* of contemporary Ireland, of 12,000,000 "profitable" acres, the Cromwellians now held 4,500,000, the old Protestants 4,000,000, and the Catholics 3,500,000; is it astonishing that there was widespread discontent?

Ormond was a Lord Lieutenant after the King's heart (1661-1668 and 1677-1685), a staunch Anglican, a staunch royalist, and completely reliable. The Catholics, being royalist in their inclinations, enjoyed underhand favor under him; he encouraged the "moderates" among them who, without mentioning the Pope, would be prepared to sign the formula that "no foreign potentate has power to release subjects from their allegiance to the Crown"; the result of his system was to leave the legal proscriptions in abeyance, and in fact to be tolerant without saying too much about it. In business matters, Ireland was treated as a colony and, as was the way with colonies in those days, her economy was subordinated and sacrificed to that of the metropolis; Westminster passed two restrictive Acts against Irish cattle, which were the most important export, and also prohibited free access to the ports of the country; exchanges by sea must pay dues to the English ports. These laws, which specially mulcted the Protestants, landlords and men of business, sowed in them the seeds of an *Irish* reaction[10] from which would grow later the notion of a nationality common to all; the laws were thus drawing together those whom policy sought to keep apart.

Neither was the interlude between Ormond's two lieutenancies nor his second term of office on the whole less favorable to Catholics. One of their leaders, Colonel Sir Richard Talbot, prevailed on London to set up a commission which, under the presidency of Prince Rupert, examined the complaints of the old families who had been dispossessed. The entry to the municipalities, from which they were excluded by law, was half opened to them. But this was all achieved stealthily and granted as a favor, not as a right; the fragile nature of the concessions can be seen in the sudden revival of anti-Catholic feeling after the conspiracy forged by Titus Oates, when Oliver Plunket, the Archbishop of Armagh, a conservative prelate and one favorable to England, was accused of high treason, on charges brought by suborned witnesses, and summarily hanged (1681).

After the accession of James II in 1685 there was a change in the atmosphere, for he was a Catholic of determined character who made no secret of his faith, a valliant sailor who wished to restore the full scope of the royal power. He created Sir Richard Talbot Duke of Tyrconnell, appointed him commander in chief and before long Lord Lieutenant (1687)—Ireland now had a Catholic viceroy! As he was the heir to an ancient

---

[10] In 1698, Molyneux, who sat as a member of the Irish Parliament for the (Protestant) University of Dublin, published *The Case of Ireland being bound by Acts of Parliament in England, stated,* in which he declared that the Irish Parliament was independent both in history and in law. This book, by orders from London, was burnt by the hangman.

Norman name, his ultimate aim was to reestablish an indigenous Assembly which should be set free from the Poynings Law and which, having supreme legislative power, could restore to the Catholics all their rights as subjects and finally revoke the Cromwellian confiscations which had been confirmed by the "Act of Settlement." (One should note that those in Ulster dating from 1611 would seem to be already too firmly established for it to be possible to contest them any longer.) Meanwhile he reinstated Catholics at the bar, in the Privy Council, and as aldermen. He raised a standing army, which was to have Catholic officers and was to uphold the King in his three kingdoms against his enemies the Whigs. Strafford's policy was once more being put into action, with all the dangers which it entailed for Ireland and which Ireland, filled with a new joy, failed to recognize.

James was driven out in November 1688 and lost Scotland at the battle of Killiecrankie; he still had Ireland, which was firmly Jacobite, but would her friends be of use to Ireland or make use of her? Tyrconnell, being an Irishman, saw clearly how things were bearing on Ireland, and there were some who even suspected him of seeking a crown. James, who was only seeking a lever to help him in his English affairs, had his eyes fixed on London. And Louis XIV, who came to the rescue, saw her as only a pawn on the European chessboard. Matters were brought to a head quickly. James, who had returned from France, landed at Kinsale (March 1689), and if Tyrconnell had men, few could be described as troops. For 40 years the population of Ireland, which in the old days used to be so warlike, had been completely disarmed and, worse still, the country, which still thought along clannish and feudal lines, had been deprived of its natural leaders, whether chieftains or lords, and was both beheaded and ground to dust. Derry, blockaded for three months (not besieged, for there was no artillery), was delivered by three ships which forced their way through in July. In August the Duke de Schomberg, a French émigré, landed 20,000 fully equipped men, and in June 1690 William of Orange arrived with his mercenaries, many of whom were Germans, bringing the total effective force up to 36,000 men. James had Lauzun's 7000 Frenchmen and the ill-equipped Irish levies. All technical superiority was on the one side; and the French Huguenots had the revocation of the Edict of Nantes to avenge. Schomberg was killed at the time of his victory. Six days later King James had left Ireland, having won there no more than an ill reputation for courage and a cruel and unpleasant nickname (Seamus an Chaca).

He had just had the time during his stay to summon a Parliament, in May 1689, and the Acts of this Assembly, though they were speedily annulled, are nevertheless of great interest, for they portray the deep thought of the nation, less what she did than what she wished. It recognized James, the *de jure* King of England, as *ipso facto* King of Ireland. It declared the Irish courts of justice to be supreme, and on its own account did away with the Poynings Law—thus greatly scandalizing James. It proclaimed religious liberty and equal rights for all subjects without any confessional distinction. It continued the tithes, with this novelty, however, that each citizen should pay for his own Church. Finally, it revoked the Act of Settlement, which had sanctioned the Cromwellian confiscations. This revocation, which was made without qualifications, would naturally cause many injustices, even if only in the case of those who had bought lands which had previously been confiscated and had paid good money for them: these were violent measures which alone could undo the results of former violent acts, counterattainders in order to annul other attainders. The worst of it was that these measures, which were to come to nothing, would on the morrow be made the pretext and the excuse for countermeasures which were far more brutal and which would remain.

The battle of the Boyne was the decisive stroke in bringing an era to an end. Already, since 1611, the greatest names in Gaelic history were to be seen setting on the horizon, the O'Donnells and the O'Neills, following the greatest names in Anglo-Norman history, the Desmonds and the Kildares. But all the same, throughout those hundred terrible years something had survived belonging to the ancient and well-beloved order; the country, with its fundamentally aristocratic tradition, had seen, in whatever party they might be, the great houses which were both her glory and her faith. The Gaelic ones with their sons Owen Roe, Inchiquin, Thomond, Claire, Antrim, Clancarthy, or the Anglo-Norman ones, like Clanricarde or Ormond, still burst into flame from the ashes and gave a dim glimmer. The men of letters, the jurists, the historians, the bards still found here and there some hospitable castle which ensured that they did not quite die of hunger. Geoffrey Keating collected the elements of Ireland's history, thanks to such patrons; the Four Masters worked at their *Annals* in their ancient Donegal shelter; and Mac Firbis was still able to write, round about 1650, his *Book of Genealogies*. After the Boyne all this system, which was even more spiritual than social, fell into ruin. This is proved by the fact that the Gaelic language, which had for so long held the supreme place, had to yield this as the speech of the aristocracy and the middle class. The Parliament of 1689 was, as may be imagined, English speaking. Another proof is that the hero of the war was Sarsfield.

It is true that on his mother's side Sarsfield was descended from the old O'Mores of Leinster; but in the paternal line he was an "old English" gentleman of the pale—though certainly always a Catholic. He had served in King Charles II's bodyguard. James, who did not like him, as he thought that he was too much concerned with Irish interests, appointed him as a brigadier with regret. Bold enterprises, as when in the first a'tack on Limerick he blew up all the enemy's ordnance, won for him a popularity which eventually became a legend. When the remains of the Irish armies withdrew into Connacht as their last stronghold, he came completely to the fore and led without faltering that long, hopeless resistance. He it was who, after the battle of Aughrim, when the French general Saint-Ruth was killed, rallied the scattered troops; he it was who, against all reason and with the technical aid of Brigadier Boisseleau, obstinately defended against Ginkel that city of Limerick of which Lauzun held that "its walls would not hold out against a battery of roasted apples"; he it was who extorted from King William the Treaty of Limerick, which gave as many safeguards as possible if only Parliament would abide by the King's word; finally it was he who embarked with his 11,000 men to serve under the white ensign and to begin that epic of the Irish Brigade which won such fame in service overseas,[11] and it was he whom exile could never rob of his last dream, that of returning

---

[11] Davis's poem should be read on their decisive charge at the battle of Fontenoy. Among the gentlemen who followed Sarsfield to France, one had the name of O'Mullally of Tullinadaly; he was the father of "Lally-Tollendal."

one day to Old Ireland and avenging her. "If only it was for Ireland," cried Sarsfield, an officer of France, when he fell on the field of Landen. A great and moving figure who bequeathed to Irish patriotism that poetic and poignant hue which from henceforth it was to have, that of unrewarded fidelity, of grief and despair.

Chapter 13.   The Penal Laws

The cheque which was signed at Limerick was not honored when presented at the bank. The treaty granted that:

(1) Catholics should enjoy the same rights as they had under Charles II;

(2) Officers or soldiers who served under King James should keep their goods and professions provided only that they took the oath of allegiance *and no other* (this protected Catholic consciences), "they themselves and all persons under their protection."

This clause, which was accepted and applied to so many people, was omitted in the copy which was presented to King William for signature; he very honestly replaced it in his own hand, but the episode was significant. In fact, from 1695 onwards, the treaty was only good for the waste-paper basket; under the impulse of the Established Church, and with the connivance of Westminster, that extraordinary structure was being erected, not unlike a pillory, which would not be complete till 1727, or abolished till 1797, one might even say 1829. Penal Laws were passed directed indiscriminately against the Catholics, some of which laid down definite pen-

alties, while there were others that were even more harm-
ful in that they were a mortgage on the future, as they
laid down disabilities.

Every Catholic priest, in order to say Mass in his parish
(and nowhere else), must be registered. A thousand
yielded to this. They were then required to take the oath
of allegiance to the Protestant succession of the Crown;
and as they naturally almost all refused to regard a
coreligionist as *a priori* unsuitable, they ceased to be
registered and thus fell back *ipso facto* into all the
dangers of illegality. No prelate was allowed to reside in
Ireland, under penalty of being hanged, drawn, and
quartered. There was a scale of premiums for informers:
£50 for a prelate who had smuggled himself in, £20
for a priest, £10 for a school master. Any priest who became a Protestant was to receive an annuity of £30, which
was to be levied on the area round his house. A Catholic
could neither carry a sword nor ride a horse worth more
than £5; his Protestant neighbor could take it from him,
after offering him £5; these regulations were all aimed at
keeping the old gentry in leading strings. No Catholic
could serve in the army or the navy, nor were they
allowed to possess arms, to vote, to be members of
Parliament or citizens of incorporated towns; they might
not live within the city boundaries of Limerick or Galway,
they were not allowed to follow the trade of an artisan
without paying a special tax known as "quarterage," they
could not have a lease of any land for more than 31
years; furthermore, any lease granted them must yield at
least two thirds of the profit to the proprietor. As the
handful of their own lawyers died out, so was the bar
closed to them. No Catholic could buy more than two
acres in the sales which followed the supreme and final
confiscation (1,100,000 acres); or acquire any land from

a Protestant neighbor, whether by sale, gift, or legacy; or leave his goods, according to the custom which ensured the continuance of families, to his eldest son, but should this eldest son become a Protestant, then he acquired an absolute right to the whole of the succession; nor could anyone, in the case of death, trust his children to anyone except a Protestant, who must bring them up in the Protestant religion. Above all, Catholics had now no means of education. For a long time Catholics who entered Trinity College had not been allowed to take degrees; they were now even forbidden to enter the college. The opening of a school was forbidden; their children would be allowed to attend the "Charter Schools," but these would train them to be Protestants. Neither were they allowed to send their children to be educated abroad. The "hedge schools," which sheer necessity brought into being, were conducted in illegal secrecy and by wandering masters—who, since they were not averse to a life of destitution and dangers, were not always of the most respectable type—and the parish priests were liable for heavy penalties in this matter. The aim was to sweep the country clear of Popery, to diminish and to grind down the faithful to the utmost limit; and, finally, if it was impossible to snatch them from their "superstition" or to exterminate them, to keep them in an absolute condition of physical and intellectual helplessness. "The Law," wrote a Lord Chancellor, "does not take into account the existence of such a person as an Irish Roman Catholic."

In order to understand the institution of the Penal Laws—I say *understand* and do not mean anything more —one must picture to oneself who the men were who passed them, and when and where they did so. The assembly in which they originated was the Dublin Parliament, to which Catholics had not been eligible since 1692 and for which, after 1727, they were no longer even electors. What did this Parliament represent? A small minority, but one which was rich from the lands it had received after the confiscation; a Church which was spoilt by opulence and which was foreign in its tradition, its language, its allegiance, and its soul. One of themselves, Fitzgibbon, could still, in 1800, describe these people with a crude candor as "the heirs of evictions, isolated in the midst of grudging masses." Being surrounded by this unreconciled populace, is it to be wondered at that they developed the mentality of besieged people? Their severity was, *mutatis mutandis,* somewhat like that of the Romans who were submerged by their crowds of slaves and lived in constant fear of an uprising. The privileged few possessed nine tenths of the land, though in numbers they were less than a quarter of the population: one in five is the figure given by one of their Lord Chancellors. Furthermore, there was in the North a compact group of dissenters, the Presbyterians, badly treated enough, too, but much less badly than the Papists; without the Presbyterians, the proportion of Anglicans would have been less than one in ten. At the same time an Anglican prelate, the Earl of Bristol (Bishop of Derry), had an income of £12,000 a year, kept a company of horsemen as his bodyguard, and used to travel across Europe with such a display of luxury that he has left his name to all the Bristol Hotels which are scattered over the Continent.

It is clear that this small minority would have been unable to defend the enormity of its privileges on its own; without support from the foreigner it would soon have collapsed, and it was thus known, in current language, as "the garrison" of this same foreigner. Conversely, England knew that she could rely on these Anglican elements to support her domination in Ireland from sheer necessity, while the Presbyterians, owing to their religion, would be unlikely to support the Catholics. Now, the England of the eighteenth century was no longer that of Charles II: in the interval there had been the revolution of 1688, the triumph of the Parliamentary oligarchy, the accession of those drunken foreigners, the Hanoverians, with the progressive eclipse of the Crown.

Anti-Catholic feeling was far stronger in the new classes who had recently come to power; whether they were Protestant or, as was often now the case, deist or rationalist, they had for one reason or the other a contempt for what they considered the Roman superstition. Parliament remembered that Ireland had risen against it three times in one century but did not try to discover the reason why; it would only look at the fact that there had been a rising, and on this ground encouraged Dublin to take repressive measures that grew worse and worse. As can be imagined, all that was achieved was to stir up the spirit of insurrection; and thus was rounded off, with monotonous and inexorable stupidity, the hellish circle of oppression and revolt.

At the same time, the strait jacket in which they were confined was gradually affecting the character of the oppressed masses. They saw how their religion, to which they clung with a firmness that increased in proportion to the efforts made to wrest it from them, was subjected to a thousand persecutions which outraged them at their most sensitive point, and they became ever more attached to their priests, of whose courage and devotion they received fresh proofs every day. They were suffering, and seemed to be without the means or the hope of any alleviation whatsoever, while the immediate

cause of their misery was the law! That can be called
law which protects, advises, raises up, and reclaims; but
what was a law which forbade them even to learn how
to read! And thus a second law came into being, which
was in reality the expression of a thwarted conscience
and was far better obeyed than the other, the fraudulent
law of the lawyers. As it was no longer possible to
wage open war, a war that would indeed be a just one,
then it must be waged underground. A secret conspiracy
would block the way of the official law. What about
informers? Their lives would be made impossible or
they would even be executed. And obdurate landlords?
They would be intimidated by night raids, by the maiming of their cattle, and be kept in a state of permanent
insecurity. And the courts of law? These could be cir-
cumvented by coalitions of witnesses, even perjury, which
could be explained away by the emergency of the situation as being no more than "white lies." And, above all,
before everything else, never a word! These habits would,
in the course of time, become implanted in the national
character and would outlive their necessity. The respect for law and the ethics of the English, in themselves
not altogether unworthy of praise, were scandalized at
these ways of the Irish; facetious Englishmen made fun
of the stereotyped "Paddy" who was always "again the
government"; but who was to blame? Who was it that
had driven the weaker side into giving these tortuous and
underground replies?

Other measures continued to injure the country; these,
which were passed in London, were of a more general
kind and spared nobody, conformist or otherwise. Men-
tion has already been made of the acts prohibiting the
export of fat cattle to England, and later export to the
colonies except through the English ports; another law

forbade the export of wool anywhere except to England, where it was burdened with a heavy tariff. Only the linen industry was spared, which had been introduced into Ireland by French refugees and which threatened no similar English industry. The Protestants were specially hit by these measures, for they were the landlords and industrialists; they were already joining forces with the Catholics in the vast smuggling activities which were made necessary by the sheer difficulties of living; and thus the conception of a possible community of interests was starting to dawn among two peoples who up to then had been antagonistic. Besides, in the North, the Presbyterians, now being thrown out of work, were sending out to the New World that smattering of emigrants which was destined to increase steadily. These men took with them their hatred as well as their destitution, and these would be remembered by them or by their sons in the coming American revolt.

NB // Macaulay says somewhere that "Ireland's slavery was the necessary condition for England's liberty." Is this more than a play upon words? For, after all, in this context, slavery means the reduction of *individuals* to the status of slaves, while liberty means the independence of the *nation:* here are two parallel planes, and one can see no point where they meet. Whatever one may think of it, this saying is the English explanation of what took place.

Chapter 14.   Underground Ireland

It was Swift, the Swift of *Gulliver* and Dean of St. Patrick's Cathedral, who first voiced the protest. This accounts for the unanimous applause with which he was welcomed, he who was a member of the minority Church, a member of the garrison: with him, the silence of the grave was being broken. Everyone repeated with pleasure the vitriolic words which were dictated by the genius of the great pamphleteer: "Ireland is the only Kingdom I have ever heard or read of, either in ancient or modern history, which was denied the liberty of exporting their native commodities wherever they pleased; yet this by the superiority of mere power is refused us. . . . Any government without the consent of the governed is the very definition of slavery; but in fact, eleven fully armed men will certainly subdue one single man in his shirt. . . . Burn everything that came from England, except their coals. . . ." Everyone appreciated the bitter irony of the *Modest Proposal* in which, in order to relieve the public destitution, Swift suggests that the little Irish children should be reared with a view to sending them to the pork butcher, quietly explaining that, as each would cost about half a crown per year, the plan would benefit everyone: the parents, the public interest, and themselves. . . .

But, in spite of everything, this savage indignation, *saeva indignatio,* which he wished to have inscribed in the epitaph still to be seen in St. Patrick's, seems to be unaware of where the injustice really lay, and to bypass the real problem. Swift seems to have no idea that the rule of the Protestants might be questioned; the original inhabitants, whose language he did not know—a language spoken all over the countryside and in every town except Dublin—these original inhabitants seemed to him a barbarous people, lawless, lazy, dirty, and sunk in superstition, in a word, not to be taken into account; and yet this was the ancient, the true, and in a sense the only Ireland. It is true that these poor outcasts had been reduced to a state of dirt and destitution and had perhaps become almost indifferent to their misery; living in cottages built of mud and thatch, which seemed to crouch on the soil, with their cattle sleeping by them, lest they should be stolen, and with a manure heap before the door, their children barefooted and in rags, themselves stupefied by misery to the point of unconsciousness, so that they no longer reacted—on this all witnesses agree.

These poor people lived on skimmed milk and potatoes; some of them even bled their cows and cooked the blood with sorrel. "The Kerry cows know when it is Sunday," runs the proverb, for on that day they were bled. One hears of wooden spades, of which the edge alone was bound with iron, while ploughs were so scarce that ploughing was a show which the whole village turned out to see; there was no harness; the plough was fastened to the horse's tail.

According to Petty, out of 180,000 houses, only 20,000 had chimneys; the smoke which filled the others caused widespread ophthalmia and resulted in a disastrous number of blind people; *dall,* "the blind," is a frequent nickname among the itinerant poets. There were 30,000 beggars on the roads. The unfortunate Irish seemed to be submerged in their wretchedness with an almost Oriental fatalism, which greatly shocked the respectability of the hard-working English. But they had every excuse. Firstly, they were originally far more a pastoral than an agricultural people, who for a thousand years had been accustomed to the slow cadence and the leisurely life of the cowherd, and instinctively they maintained the same outlook. Besides, as they were permanently undernourished, it was weakness which caused the tools to fall from their hands: if one may believe Corkery, 400,000 people died in the 1740 famine. And then, if they appeared to be idle, maybe it was the carelessness of despair; there seemed to be no escape from their fate.

And one can well understand their concluding so. Their landlord would usually be one of those noblemen who lived in London, one of the absentee landlords, of whom there were about a hundred, rich possessors of immense demesnes or rather territories which they had inherited from the confiscations; in the last one alone, James II, who was still Duke of York, had received 70,000 acres, while the Duke of Ormond, over and above his already enormous palatinate, received 100,000. The traffic was one-way only; all the rents went to England, without coming back in the form of investments. These magnates scarcely ever visited their lands; they belonged to this people neither in race nor in language; they were unable to enter into that human relationship, often of an affectionate nature, which in England linked the squire and his tenants as a rule. What they were looking for was money, and to have it without bother. They entrusted their affairs to an agent, who was often in charge of several estates, and if he found himself overworked he would make use of a number of local subagents, who in their turn had their baliffs—these occasionally half peasants and Catholics!—to squeeze from the poor the last ounce of their substance. The ass's back broken down under such an avalanche of intermediaries.

The rent was at the landlord's wish, there being more applicants than farms to be given; since the demand exceeded the supply, there was a plethora of laborers, with no alternative work (there was scarcely any industry) and with the permanent threat of eviction. Even in Protestant Ulster, a Marquis of Donegal, having given the order on the expiration of the leases that a further £100,000 was to be raised on his estate, at one blow put thousands of farmers on the roads. Everything was working against the peasant: the Enclosure Act, which was applied as in England, cut off the common lands on which he had always held the right of pasturage and collecting wood; the circumstances that as there was a demand for meat in England, the landlords turned the ploughland into ranches and drove out the human beings to make room for the cattle; the hearth tax, which sounds small enough at two shillings per fire but took a week's work to raise. Being closely watched by the bailiff who, being on the spot, knew everything and at the first sign of small improvements made fresh demands on him, the unfortunate peasant went to ground and did not stir. There was a premium on his idleness.

And then he belonged to a tradition of his own, an original tradition which he could not give up and which, when compared with the other, he greatly preferred. He suffered all the more keenly from this deprivation of his rights, which he knew to be undeserved, in that he had within him a secret pride, for he still knew that he was one of *Clann na nGael,* a child of the Gaels. He did not admit the superiority of his conquerors; and what he felt more deeply than his destitution was their contempt. His own tradition was essentially aristocratic and patriarchal, content with inequality and indeed based on it, in which the humble man took pride by proxy in the greatness of his princes, as long as they were the right ones. What had happened to them now, the O'Neills, O'Donnells, O'Connors, MacCarthys, O'Briens? They were serving under foreign standards, and their castles were empty or had been usurped. Who was left to honor and to care for the poets, the trustees of those ancient memories in which a whole people had shared since the earliest ages and which, from the highest prince down to the lowliest of the *spailpíní*, made them to be one?[12] For—in this the English had made no mistake—what continued to stir up this resistance, which in its weakness was nevertheless inextinguishable, was—and here was the marvel!—poetry and the poets; it was the lore of ideas, of legends and customs which had survived through them and was still keeping up the fight. So deep was this instinct that it united not only castle and cottage, as indeed it had always done, but even the two extremes of the day, Catholic and Protestant: one Pierce Fitzgerald, an Anglican (perhaps against his will), was singing in Gaelic the praises of the Blessed Virgin.

There still remained, in forgotten corners, some ancient Gaelic families—the O'Connells of Derryname are typical of these—who continued to live the patriarchal life of the days gone by, poor in money but rich in things, self-sufficient in their rough plenty, and who, as they spoke Gaelic, remained more or less able to preserve without ostentation some of the ancient tradition. It was, no doubt, thanks to such people that there were bardic schools still in existence in the eighteenth century, such as are described in the *Memoirs* of the Marquis of Clanricarde (1722); young men were to

[12] It is difficult to imagine how tenacious such a tradition could be which, on the threshold of modern times, was still full of the spirit of the middle ages. A history of love and magic (with the lover changed into a werewolf) which was written in Norman in the thirteenth century by William of Palermo and translated into English in the XVth century, the age of the *Morte d'Arthur*, was rendered in Irish round about 1680, for some prince fond of such tales.

be seen coming together from all over Ireland to be taught by a master and along with him to live by the liberality of the neighborhood; in the morning a common subject would be proposed, and then each student would shut himself up in his cell, which would be deliberately kept dark, and lie motionless on his bed, often with a stone on his chest, composing with an astonishing intentness. In the evening each one would recite his composition, and finally everyone, both master and disciples, would come together to take part in a general criticism. This intensive form of training lasted for years, as the language used by that professional literature was frequently archaic and the meters extremely complex, both calling for the most assiduous efforts if they were to be mastered thoroughly.

And then the flame began to sink for lack of oil. Those masters who lacked the patronage of some great house had to take to the spade in order to live. But the need remained and expressed itself in those "Courts of Poetry" wherein the bards used to assemble, brought together by a message from one of the elders; they would meet in a cottage, at a crossroads, or even in a public house. The poetry, which had found its way down the steps from the castle to the farm, had changed. The old syllabic meters, which were so difficult and so scholarly, had been replaced by the new *amhráin,* which was based on the accent, and the upholders of the tradition were indignant: "What, poetry without a darkened room! Without painful ordeals!" The tone changed, as did the subjects: instead of the everlasting combats, alliances, genealogies, and funeral laments, it now expressed the master's sadness at the loss of his old gray horse which had died, or else consisted of elegies about the dark Rosaleen, which is Ireland, or about the lover for whom

she waits in vain, which is the far-away Stuart. In three
generations of poets one can sense the profound and
rapid changes which were taking place around them.
The first, Egan O'Rahilly (1665-1726), still belongs
completely to that ancient world which was the heir of
the centuries, in which the great names were everything,
and his lament is over the exile or the eclipse of his
MacCarthy princes. Owen Roe O'Sullivan (1748-1784)
still makes use of the traditional literary terms, but he
is a kind of Villon, whether schoolmaster or laborer, a
bit of a rogue, the mere peasant, and he has produced
no verse about the noblemen departed. Brian Merriman
(1750-1805) uses the common dialect as spoken round
him by the people of Clare in his work *The Midnight
Court* which, while it still has a fairylike quality, is at
the same time racy and rustic. One finds, however, that
one Michael Comyn, Protestant though he is, reverts
in harmonious strains to the very ancient legend of
Ossian marrying the daughter of the King of the Waves
and, centuries later, returning from Tir na nÓg, the
country of eternal youth, to a Christian Ireland which
he no longer recognizes (1758).

These "men of poetry" had neither newspapers nor
books nor printing press; and the marvelous thing is
that the people knew their poems by heart. The poor
man, in his dark, unsanitary hovel, if he heard a line
sung, burst with delight; he and his neighbors met in the
evenings to compare and exchange the treasures of their
memories; I myself, not more than ten years ago, heard
an old man of 80 in the wilds of Kerry, on hearing the
name of Finn, pour out like a cataract the torrent of
verse that he kept in his head. Having no means of
printing, they copied the poems. If his copy was a
scrawl, the scribe would lay the blame on the bad light,

which was provided by the turf fire, or at the best by improvised candles made from reeds. . . . The poets themselves worked, hoe in hand, all day long in order to earn their pittance of twopence or fourpence or even, as in Galway, which was an opulent town, of as much as sixpence a day; at nightfall they "became themselves once more," as O'Sullivan expresses it; in his case he would repair to his own self, that of Owen Roe of the Melodious Mouth. And this struggle for the soul of the land was to go well on into the nineteenth century. So great was the love that this people at bay had for their language and their poetry, the need that they had of it and for the link that it forged between them all. Such was the ancient and the true Ireland, the tragic Ireland whose agony only persisted because, for so long and with such fervent desire, she was determined that she would not die.

III. THE "PROTESTANT NATION"

Chapter 15. The Great Days and the Decadence ·of the "Garrison"

In 1714 Anne of England was about to die. The rightful heir was clearly the Stuart, James III, son of King James, dethroned in 1688; he was at the time Louis XIV's guest at Saint Germain; Bolingbroke was secretly on his side. He was, however, overthrown by the *coup d'état* which brought Shrewsbury to power and the Electors of Hanover to the throne; these were descended from James I on the female side and had the hereditary name of George. These princes recognized the supremacy of Parliament both in fact and by right, which meant that they were under the thumb of the Whig oligarchy in control: *by right,* because, in receiving the crown, they accepted the "glorious revolution" of 1688; *in fact,* because, being foreigners even in language, they were incapable of taking a real part in the affairs of the nation and indeed had no wish to do so, and so for two generations they were to be mere puppet kings. Ireland, which had the tradition of appealing from the severity of Parliament to the "King's Grace," had nothing to hope for

91

from such walkers-on; on the other hand, she was only too well aware of the powerlessness of the Pretender: the Duke of Ormond who, though a Protestant, was a partisan of James, had been sentenced by attainder and went to die in exile (1745). Such lessons were not lost on the Irish, and this explains why, though Jacobite by instinct, Ireland did not raise a finger for the "King across the water," either in 1715 or 1745.

One cannot indeed fail to notice that for half a century political Ireland was merely one great silence. The Catholics, whether of peasant stock or bearing a great name, seemed to be definitely brought down and even resigned, while the Protestant population, which was not considered reliable, was now systematically ousted from positions. The "English by blood" found themselves inexorably governed by those who were "English by birth," and it was among them that the first signs of opposition were to be found which, though at first they were but slight, were to gather weight in the future. For the time being, on the one hand, the Established Church was to be found imposing its control equally on the Papists and on the dissident Presbyterians or Dissenters;[13] on the other hand, though in appearance the country was administered by viceroys representing the Crown, it was in fact governed by Anglican prelates appointed by London, such as Boulter (1724-1742) and Stone (1742-1764), both Protestant Archbishops of Armagh and Primates of all Ireland, who ruled in their capacity as Lords-Justice. The state of affairs was thus one of foreign rule in which a foreign Church, which was further-

---

[13] It is true that an Act of Toleration granted them liberty of conscience in 1719; but it was London which forced the Anglican Church in Ireland to make this concession, and the Dissenters continued to be excluded from positions.

more well packed with foreign personnel, took part in the administration in the foreign interest; a protectorate in all but name. In other words, one could describe it as government by two stages, in which the Established Church governed Ireland and the Cabinet governed the Established Church. The system, which before all else made sure of the subjection of Ireland, was formally established by George I's Declaratory Act in 1719, which

(1) refused the status of Supreme Court of Appeal for the country to the Irish House of Lords;

(2) made the laws passed at Westminster binding on the Kingdom of Ireland.

It may seem surprising that such an Act should be passed without opposition in Dublin, by an Irish House, but one must remember how that House was composed. Firstly, it was representative only of the Protestant minority, and even of the officially Protestant one, since only that section of the population could elect or be elected. Furthermore, even within that section the "rotten" and "pocket" borough held sway; some constituencies had a few electors, others had none, and always "belonged" to "patrons." And then, in the Parliament itself, in Dublin as in London, majorities could be bought by means of titles, pensions and sinecures, with the worsening effect that, whereas in England it was the government which did the buying, here it was done by "undertakers" who made a business out of it for themselves; the most influential among them were Malone, Boyle, and (*quantum mutatus ab illis!*) the Earl of Kildare. This Parliament did not even have a regular period of duration; having once been elected, it was there for the whole of the reign, and that of George II lasted thirty-two years. The Lord-Lieutenant or viceroy, nominal head of the government, was in fact a high

official who took his orders from the English Home
Secretary; he was not even a resident and only appeared
occasionally in order to preside over the sessions. Such
was the apparatus which made Ireland "safe" for the
"imperial Crown" and for the "Protestant Constitution."

At a lower level the Catholics, who were without civic
or personal rights, were growing still weaker, not so
much because of desertions (it is reckoned that 5000
families joined the Protestant Church between 1703 and
1788 in order to save their estates, which is not many)
but through divergencies of interest and consequently of
attitude. The few great houses which had not been submerged and the middle class of the towns thought it
wisest to go quietly and to aim at what concessions they
could, while loudly proclaiming their loyalty. The
"Catholic Committee" and the higher clergy, who had
learned through disastrous experiences, were above all
concerned with obtaining the government's connivance
at the existence of an organized Church, and followed a
more or less similar policy; they accepted, for instance,
the Act of Allegiance of 1774, which specifically denied
that the Pope had any temporal power or the right to
depose princes. There was, however, a somber under-
world in which the peasants, exasperated by the in-
tolerable conditions under which they had to live, conspired together in rather weak terrorist bands known as
the Whiteboys; thus began that long series of outrages
and acts of intimidation, the driving and maiming of
cattle and all the rest, which for more than a century
were to be a constant feature of the agrarian struggle.

Up above, in the broad daylight of the official world,
the first ripple appeared on the still waters. A bill was
sent from London appropriating some Irish surplus
revenue, but the Dublin Parliament refused to pass it;

it denied that the King had the right to dispose of the
national money, and claimed this right for itself. An arrangement was as usual come to with the leaders: Boyle,
the President of the House, was made Earl of Shannon,
Malone became Lord Chancellor, and the Earl of Kildare was made Duke of Leinster. Such were the beginnings, though perhaps rather inglorious ones, of the
"patriot party." Nevertheless they were beginnings.

George III, who succeeded to the Crown in 1760, was
a king; he was born an Englishman, he spoke English,
and he wished to take his part in public affairs; while
he wished well to *all* his subjects, there were limits to
his benevolence, for he considered himself to be bound
in conscience by his religion and his oath to "constitutional monarchy." He sent Lord Townshend as viceroy
in 1767, with orders to be resident—and thus gave to
Dublin the splendor of a capital, which from that day
to this it has never lost—and also to satisfy reasonable
claims. London had every reason to be pleased with Ireland, by which it had been loyally served during the
Seven Years' War. In reward, the duration of the
Dublin Parliament was from then onwards fixed at eight
years. The buying of votes was withdrawn from the
"undertakers" and reserved to the government itself;
this showed perhaps but little progress in morality, but
it was a real step forward in public order. Opinion was
slowly changing in their favor in regard to the Catholics.
Religious hatreds were cooling down, not because of an
increase in charity but rather because of the increase
of contemporary scepticism. Over in America the horizon was growing dark. The unimpeachable "loyalty" of
the Catholic upper class and of the hierarchy did the
rest. Everything was in favor of emancipating the Catholics, anyway from the penal section of the laws directed

against them; as for their disabilities, if once they were annulled, doubts might be cast on the property rights of many a Protestant family. Various measures of relief followed first in practice alone (as under Lord Chesterfield, at the time of Culloden) and then in the laws themselves, against those restrictions which had weighed on them up to then: in 1778, by the Gardiner Law, they were enabled to enter upon leases of indefinite length, to inherit and to bequeath property in the usual way, according to the law of primogeniture.

From then onwards the tide was on the ebb. The war in America had been going badly since 1775. London had need of the numerous troops (12,000 men) who were stationed in Ireland and paid by her; the sympathies of Ireland, for obvious reasons, were with the other side; these people must therefore be coaxed over. Finally, the Parliamentary opposition had been reinforced by two new arrivals who were making themselves heard and were eclipsing the old hands; these were Henry Flood, a man of cold character, methodical and incisive, who still belonged definitely to the "Protestant Nation" but demanded that she should be given the admission of her independence in black and white; Grattan, who had a warmer soul, and whose eloquence was of a florid type, would gladly have obtained full civilian rights for the Catholics. At least, in 1782, a second Gardiner Law swept aside all the remaining laws which could, strictly speaking, be called penal; Catholics could now purchase, lend, possess, and make wills in exactly the same way as the Protestants, the secular clergy were officially freed from the need of registration, the regular clergy were authorized to take up residence and the laity to bear arms, while their children could receive instruction.

The danger in which England found herself increased the pace; she had to capitulate at Yorktown, and Ireland lay exposed; if France were to land an expeditionary force, who knew whether the peasants, even the Presbyterians among them, would not rise, simply out of hatred for their execrated landlords? When the "patriot party" suggested raising volunteers for the defense of the country, London accepted the offer and armed them. There were before long 80,000 men on foot, commanded in the North by Lord Charlemont, in the South by the Duke of Leinster. But here was a force with which Flood and Grattan had every intention of pressing for the rights of Ireland, the "sister nation," as Swift had called her, and no longer a slave. From then onwards, rights had behind them the support of arms. In February 1782 the Convention or Assembly of Dungannon proclaimed as "unconstitutional and illegal every attempt to make laws which bind the Kingdom unless by the King and the Lords and Commons of Ireland," and specifically challenged "the powers exercised by the Privy Councils of both Kingdoms in virtue of the Poynings Law." In May, the reformist Whigs at Westminster, under the aegis of Burke and Fox, revoked the famous Declaratory Act of 1719. There was much enthusiasm in Dublin. "Ireland is now a nation," cried Grattan: "In that new character I hail her, and bowing before her august presence, I say: *Esto perpetua!*" finally, on January 22, 1783, Westminster solemnly carried a bill which declared that Ireland was "bound only by the laws that should be passed by His Majesty and the Parliament of that Kingdom, and this is now established and acknowledged for all time, and shall never be called in question."

Chapter 16. The "Protestant Nation"

The years which followed left behind them the memory
of a period which was beneficial, prosperous, and glorious. And, indeed, the traces of it can still be found on
the face of Ireland, in the canals, with their quiet, old-
fashioned charm, which cross the country from one sea
to the other, and in the beautiful buildings with which
Dublin is embellished, whether public, such as the Four
Courts and the Custom House, or private, such as Leinster House, which is now occupied by the Dail, or
Charlemont House, now a picture gallery; these buildings are reminiscent of Tourny's work in Bordeaux,
and they have about them an atmosphere of elegance
and magnificence, a reflection of the aristocratic spirit
of the time. The truth is that during those eighteen years
when Ireland had a national Parliament, her prosperity
grew by leaps and bounds; the population seems to have
increased by a quarter; the weaving of wool and cotton
was encouraged and in a flourishing state, as were also
the glass factories of Waterford; above all, the Foster
Law, which continued to be the charter of the country
till 1846, practically forbade the importation of foreign corn; because of this law the ocean of grass was
turned into cornfields, which gave steady work to the
farm laborers and also produced profitable exports to
England. And yet this happy period was very short-
lived; why was this?

To understand why, one must distinguish and follow
a number of threads which together form a very tangled
skein. To begin with, the age, which was one of transi-
tion, still retained the cleavages which it had inherited

from the past, like that between the Catholics and the
Protestants, and there were a number of other cleavages
as well, most of them due to fresh factors, such as the
revolutions in France and America and the abolition of
privileged classes. Nor must we forget that Grattan's
Parliament, though so attractive in retrospect, was in no
sense representative; it could only be entered by Protestants belonging to the Established Church, who made up
about one tenth of the population, and even in speaking
of this tenth, one is not giving a true picture; of three
hundred members, two thirds were chosen by "patrons,"
the proprietors of "rotten boroughs," and at least half of
those elected were "place men," people who were fatten-
ing themselves in positions which they owed to the
government (some were not even residents, and lived
on their sinecures in London), and who would in consequence vote at the beck and call of the Castle. And
then the beloved and revered "Constitution of 1782"
was the most extraordinary hybrid in the world; the
Irish Parliament was certainly a sovereign assembly,
since it was founded on the royal will and not on any
vote at Westminster, but it controlled no Irish government, since there was none. The government of the country was in theory in the hands of the viceroy, appointed
by the British Cabinet, and in fact no more than their
agent. Thus it was that Pitt, the English Prime Minister,
found himself faced with a strange monstrosity, worse
even than a creature with two heads, for it had one
head and two bodies.

Any sensible person could see that the system would
not really work and that it must be altered, for example
by making the assembly a more faithful picture of the
nation. But *which* nation? The *Protestant* nation, answered Flood, who was anti-Catholic, but a democrat in

his strange way, and who only wished to enlarge the
electorate (which should be Protestant, of course) to
increase the number of truly elected members at the
expense of those who in practice were nominated, and
thus to induce corruption from without. The *whole* nation, answered Grattan, who was pro-Catholic but an
aristocrat, and who dreamt of giving Catholics the right
to vote, of admitting their upper classes to Parliament,
and hoped by Parliamentary reforms to reduce corruption from within. But apart from them was one
Wolfe Tone, who despised them both. Low born, without
religion (except the vague deism of the age), the son of
two revolutions, that of America and that of France, he
was intoxicated with the Rights of Man and of the Citizen, and wished to combine all the underdogs, whoever
they were, Presbyterians or Catholics, all the oppressed,
against the ruling caste, and to establish holy equality
through the medium of his United Irishmen; he did not
make his appeal to the Catholic masses as Papists, whom
he scorned, but as potential insurgents, whom he required. At the other extreme, one finds John Fitzgibbon,
Earl of Clare, who before long became Chancellor, the
very soul of the clique who ruled in the Castle; coming,
as he did, of ancient Norman Catholic stock and being
the son of a transfuge, he had, as such, to prove doubly
"loyal"; along with Westmoreland, the viceroy, he defined the government as "a Protestant garrison holding
the land, the magistracy and the power in the country,
the position of which was guaranteed by British power
and supremacy, and which was always ready to crush
any rising among the vanquished." These words were
clear enough, and the corollary which necessarily followed was that the Protestant oligarchy depended on the

imperial link; if this was threatened there was only one remedy, that of absorption or "Union." Finally, at the apex of everything stood Pitt, the leader of the executive, the head of the Cabinet who found himself faced with two independent, equal Parliaments, an odd and perilous situation.

This danger was brought home to him by two episodes. In 1784 he proposed a commercial treaty which was favorable to Ireland; Dublin said yes, but Westminster altered the scheme in an adverse direction, whereupon Dublin said no. In 1788 George III had an attack of insanity. Westminster claimed the right to appoint the Prince of Wales as Regent, while restricting him within certain limits; Dublin, however, claimed that it recognized him on its own account, without any reservations, and that anyway it would accept no King of Ireland from London. These deadlocks between two sovereign powers, which he seemed to have no means of avoiding, gave Pitt food for thought. In the midst of this, Grattan, who was the soul of integrity and feared lest he should be suspected of underhand dealing, refused to enter the government; this was a serious mistake, for it meant leaving Pitt to Fitzgibbon's influence, the latter being supreme at the Castle. Besides, Pitt soon found himself faced (from 1793 onwards, after the rupture with France) by a war to the death with France, and from then on he was to sacrifice everything to the task of waging the war, as was his job. Now, Ireland had four and a half million inhabitants and Britain eight; the Irish peasants, accustomed to a hard life, were born soldiers, and large numbers of them were to be found in the British regiments; a disaffected Ireland would have been very dangerous. When faced with so many doubtful elements, the conclusion which was reached, whether wrongly or rightly, was that it was not possible to have confidence in Ireland or to satisfy her, but merely to hold her. If one keeps in mind how many diverse interests there were, interwoven with one another, one can understand how inexorable was the drift towards the tragedy of insurrection, with its unavoidable result, the Union.

The decisive step was taken in January 1795. Lord Fitzwilliam had been appointed viceroy, a man whose sympathies lay with Grattan and the Catholics and who had instructions to try and win them over. Such a policy naturally required that the Castle should be purged of its reactionary junta, which would otherwise be certain to block everything; but Pitt declared himself resolutely opposed to Fitzgibbon's dismissal, and Fitzwilliam was cast aside. When he left, the streets of Dublin were draped in black as the viceroy's carriage drove through. Tone took ship for France, for he now believed only in arms. The iron die had been cast.

For, once such a policy had been adopted, the inevitable consequences would follow. Every attempt at parliamentary reform was opposed, for it was clear that a shadow assembly such as this, dominated by its fear of the excluded Catholics, would be easier to handle than a real one and could be bribed or, if need be, coerced. The nation must, above all things, be prevented from being compact, and the inspiring idea of a united Ireland must be nipped in the bud; that is why, in that very Ulster where it came to birth, by stirring up dissensions between the rival tenants the Castle set the "Peep of Day Boys," who were Presbyterians, against the "Defenders," who were Catholics, and thus caused brawls which soon led to murders, man hunts, and the

exodus of terrified populations;[14] that is why, on the
other hand, much was being made of the Catholic conservatives and the bishops, who were hostile to the
French revolution; Maynooth was founded, the seminary
intended to replace their continental houses which had
been closed during the storm; glittering promises of
emancipation, in return for their support, were held out
to them. Finally, forceful measures were necessary so
as to be ready for the upheaval when it came, either by
disarming it beforehand or else using a provocative re-
pressiveness so as to make it go off at halfcock. The
Parliament of the privileged minority was almost overwhelmed with alarm, as it listened to the underground
rumblings in which the resentments of the past were
strangely mingled with the new revolutionary enthusiasm; its members, bought by the Castle, were ready to
go to any lengths in their own defense. With the Castle's
connivance the Volunteers were disbanded, and in their
place was raised a militia completely devoted to the
government, which soon numbered 15,000 men, and
then a yeomanry, exclusively Protestant and consisting
of 50,000 partisans boiling over with hatred, who were
set loose on the country, backed by 15,000 regular
troops. As soon as they were in position, these people
first received the order to disarm Ulster, which was considered to be the most dangerous area. Two generals
of honorable character, Cornwallis, the same man who
had been vanquished at Yorktown, and Abercrombie,
who had previously served in Ireland, refused to take

---

[14] This was the time when the Orange Order first came into being;
they took their name from King William, the victor of the Boyne,
and formed a secret armed society which had as its aim the
maintenance of the legal Protestant supremacy and the spirit of
which, in our day, lay behind Ulster separatism (1920).

part. Abercrombie declared that the army was "in a state of indiscipline which made it a danger to everyone except the enemy." A third, Lake, undertook the office of executioner. Under him there was widespread rape and torture (and, be it noted, the Presbyterians were the chief victims); but he was able to reap a harvest of 50,000 muskets and 70,000 pikes (1797). Then did the tragedy follow out its inexorable course.

Tone, received by Carnot and made a French Adjutant-General, was at last able to convert Paris to the idea of making an attack in Ireland. The moment was a suitable one; the mutiny at the Nore, in which a number of Irish took part, having been "pressed" into the service against their will, had weakened the enemy's navy. On the other hand, the French navy was, to its misfortune, lacking in suitable ship's officers, for these had emigrated to a man. This was the cause of the reverse met with by Hoche, who came from Brest with 15,000 men, and arms as well, but was so badly knocked about by the storm that he had to return from Bantry without firing one shot. Another expedition, which was prepared in the Texel with the ships of the Batavian Republic, was in August 1798 overwhelmed by Admiral Duncan at the battle of Camperdown. In the meantime, Grattan, who was in despair, had for the last time entreated that the Catholic masses should be appeased by granting them adequate representation, and when his appeal was rejected, had left the House; what the Assembly, in its fear and its hatred, desired, was a repression that would strike terror into the population. The rising was sporadic and disjointed, for it was headless; its headquarters had been taken unawares, the brothers Sheares hanged, and Lord Edward Fitzgerald dead from a wound he had received when defending himself.

It is a strange fact that the insurrection was at its most widespread and formidable in the County Wexford, which was to a large extent populated with former immigrants from Western England and Brabant, and one of the least Gaelic counties in the island. It was a tale of pikes against artillery, of desperate courage against discipline and arms. Two priests led their men, Fathers Michael Murphy and John Murphy, as well as a Protestant landlord who had espoused their cause, Bagenal Harvey. All three perished. The defeat at Vinegar Hill settled the fate of the rising. Acts of cruelty had been perpetrated by both sides; on the one hand, they were the acts of uneducated peasants driven to desperation, on the other the result of a carefully thought out policy of terrorism, which was to leave behind it a long and dreadful trail of bitterness. Once again the French arrived—after the battle. Humbert and his thousand men were without difficulty able to dispose of Lake's undisciplined troops at "the Races of Castlebar," but they were surrounded by Cornwallis with overwhelming numbers, and capitulated. A little later Wolfe Tone was captured on board the *Hoche* and, as he was denied the honor of being shot, cut his throat so as to avoid the gallows. The incident was closed.

All that remained was to achieve that on which Pitt had already decided, the Union. It was the only way of preventing what they had already seen from happening again in the future, collusion between Ireland and the enemy. It was, on the other hand, in his thought, the *sine qua non* of Catholic emancipation; for, in Westminster, they would be so heavily outnumbered that they would constitute no danger. In January 1799 the prelates, assembled at Maynooth under the chairmanship of Dr. Troy, accepted the State subsidies but in

return had to recognize the government's right to be
consulted in the nomination of bishops.¹ It is worthy
of remark, for it shows how much repugnance there
was in the country, that the Dublin Parliament, servile
as it was, resisted the Union project for a whole year.
Cornwallis, who was now viceroy, and proposed it, to
begin with had to retreat before Grattan. Men had either
to be worn down or else to be bought. Out of 300 members, 72 holding positions which were revocable were
at the mercy of the Castle; the proprietors of 84 "rotten
boroughs" could be indemnified, and 28 members of
the House were raised to the peerage. It cost more than
a million pounds—which went furthermore to Ireland's
debit—to buy the Parliament but on June 7, 1800, the
Union was passed. Ireland was to send to the British
Houses 100 members and 28 peers, and as the Catholics were excluded through the Oath of Allegiance to
the Protestant succession, they became electors without
being eligible. There was to be free trade between the
two countries. The burden of imperial expense was to
be borne in the proportion of two on one side and fifteen
on the other, while the military occupation was well able
to muzzle public opinion. "Ireland is on fire," Lord
Camden had said. "We must either extinguish it or else
cut the cable and allow her to drift away." The fire ship
was now extinguished. Pitt remained faithful to his
ideas, once the deed was done, and proposed the complete enfranchisement of the Catholics, who should be
admitted to Parliament and to public positions. The
aged King, however, once more assailed by his usual
scruples, said that such a thing would be contrary to the
oath he had taken on the day of his coronation, and that
he wished to hear no more about it.

IV.   MODERN
TIMES

Chapter 17.   O'Connell

Pitt, who was aware that France, regicide and impious and the jailer of the Pope, was an object of horror to the Irish episcopate, dreamt of making the latter the pillar of British rule, through the granting of concessions. In 1808, and again in 1813, the Cabinet offered the eternal temptation, that of giving favors to the Catholic Church on consideration of its having control in the choice of bishops. The prelates were inclined to say yes; Mgr. Quarantotti, the Prefect of Propaganda, in the name of Rome was urging them to do so; the project, which would in fact have enslaved the Church to the profit of the government, came to nothing because of the spirited intervention of a young barrister: Daniel O'Connell.

O'Connell was a Gael of the Gaels, who had spoken Gaelic from his earliest days and who had even been brought up in a Gaelic cottage, through the ancient custom of "fosterage." His family, who had been robbed of their possessions in the Cromwellian confiscations, found a refuge in a remote corner of Kerry, Derrynane, where they achieved prosperity by smuggling and lived a patriarchal life, that of the clan, a life of simplicity and at the same time of plenty: when Montalembert went there in 1831, he found 120 people at the chieftain's table. And yet, while this family home was a survival of the most ancient and authentic indigenous tradition, it also shared to the full in the modern spirit; through its sons, who flew away regularly in order to serve with the Irish Brigade, it kept in close touch with the Continent. It was from this that Daniel derived the color of his thought, which—minus irreligion—is so much redolent of the eighteenth century and the "enlightenment," of a cosmopolitan tendency free from nationalism, of a horror of violence and bloodshed which reminds one of Voltaire, and a thoroughly rationalistic indifference to the inspiration that dwelt in the old ancestral language, "an obstacle to progress." The man was out of the ordinary, handsome, with an imposing presence and a voice like thunder that, in the open air, could reach, allure, and captivate crowds without number, and also with a gift for organization and an acute knowledge of his people; in short, in the true sense of the word, the born demagogue, the first leader since Sarsfield in whom old Ireland could fully recognize a son.

He was, like Burke, anti-revolutionary, and to that extent anti-French; his idea of liberty was of a more British type; what he had in view was the liberty, or rather the liberties, of the Irishman, not the independence of the Irish nation; he was a monarchist who, though he continued to be the leader of an opposition, was most sincere in his attachment to the Crown, to which he bore witness on many occasions; he merely wished that it should be more truly the Crown of Ireland. He started off faced with three problems, the system under which the land was held, autonomous government, religious discrimination, and it was the last of these that he attacked first—under historical conditions which we must recall if we would do justice to his effort.

Of the two interpretations of the fact of the Union, the one which Fitzgibbon and not Pitt had in mind was rapidly insisted on: that a garrison, supported by English backing, should keep "the former inhabitants of the island" in the position which had been assigned to them, such was the exact aim followed by those in power. Every attempt to alter the vested interests met with the most furious resistance in London; the sentiment expressed by the old war cry of "No popery!" was very active once again; an absolute, mulish resistance was to be met with especially in the Upper House, in which a number of Lords were Irish landowners on a large scale; the Orange order also kept its menace constantly suspended; it had 125,000 members with a royal prince at their head. The power of the landlords, already so great in a country where almost the only work to be found was on the land, had been increased yet further by the Act of 1816, which facilitated evictions—half in the spirit of the age, for which the right of ownership was never thought safe enough, half in remembrance of 1798, a recurrence of which must at all cost be prevented. In 1815 Sir Robert Peel had established the Royal Irish Constabulary, commonly known as the Peelers, a police force very numerous in proportion to the population and also well armed, being more of an occupying force than anything else, with the special duty of keeping a close watch and suppressing the slightest sign of disobedience. Beneath this machinery of repression, which ensured her silence, Ireland was suffering; her industry, which was still that of craftsmen, was unable to hold its own against the concentration of capital and the steam engines which were already at work in England; in 1824 certain protective rights, which had been provided for at the time of the Union, disappeared, and this meant yet another disaster; as the debt caused by the Napoleonic wars was ruining the Irish exchequer, the two treasuries were amalgamated, but the country had then no longer any say in the uses to which its money was put. The sufferings of the social body revealed themselves in the outrages committed here and there by the Ribbonmen, to which London replied with the law prohibiting assemblies, the suspension of *habeas corpus,* and the various coercion measures which were applied to the symptoms but failed to attack the root of the evil.

The real evil was the unspeakable misery in which a whole peasantry was kept and left to decay. At least, during the 22 years of war, the high price of corn had given a great stimulus to tillage and had provided work and wages; *pari passu* with this, rents had risen, even to an imprudent extent—but can one be imprudent when starving? With the end of hostilities, these artificial conditions collapsed; grass and cattle, which were more profitable, once again reduced the number of cornfields, and evictions became ever more frequent— this it was which produced those hidden attempts at revenge and the atmosphere of conspiracy. This peasantry so ill treated, so simple and unlettered and lacking in any chance to be otherwise, hard pressed as it was by the most desperate want, at the same time preserved in its deepest self the memory of its ancestors and a pride in what they had been, combined with a profound bitterness at the wrong which was being done to them.

And then, as so often happens in extreme poverty, the population was increasing at a dangerous rate, so that between the years 1800 and 1847 it was almost doubled; it now numbered more than eight and a half millions. There had been a minor famine in 1817 and a worse one in the years 1821-1822. It was out of these helpless, despairing masses, who were unorganized and so enslaved to their landlords that they had to vote at their behest, that O'Connell was to raise a force which would be feared and to forge a weapon of war.

To be a Catholic was the mark of a slave, and it was precisely on this that he was to build. In virtue of an act which had been passed in former days by Grattan's Parliament, through fear of the Volunteers, which forbade all political assemblies other than Parliament, the Catholic Committee was suppressed. Daniel O'Connell then founded the Catholic Association of 1823, with rules which were cleverly drawn up to prevent it coming under the legal ban. He was a skillful lawyer and prided himself that he could drive a coach-and-six through any act of Parliament. And he looked to the clergy for support: not so much to the hierarchy, who were inclined to be too conservative and prudent and whom on one or two occasions he had no hesitation in opposing (he relied still less on the great lords and rich Catholics, such as the Kenmares and the Fingalls), but to the humble parish clergy, men of peasant stock, who were now educated in Ireland and lived in close contact with the people. It was through them that he was able to weave the strong net which he cast over Ireland and which made him her master—so much her master that he himself was assailed by scruples and wondered whether his position was not unlawful and unconstitutional; it was they who were able to persuade the poor people to give out of their poverty one penny a month, the "Catholic rent," which brought in an income of £50,000 a year; it was they who inspired them with the courage to vote without heeding their landlords' orders, even at the risk of starvation. Then and thus was consummated again the profound union between the Irish people and their Church. It was a sign of the times that in the elections of 1826 Lord George Beresford, to his astonishment, found himself defeated in County Waterford, most of which was owned by his family. The famous Clare election followed in 1828. O'Connell was elected, refused to take the anti-Catholic oath of 1692, was excluded and reelected. Wellington, who was Prime Minister, thought he was faced with civil war, and yielded. Catholic Emancipation had been won (1829).

But it was in theory rather than in fact. The men of the Castle continued to keep the positions of authority for their Protestant coreligionists, while in London the property qualification of forty shillings (which gave 100,000 people the right to vote) was raised to £10, so as to lessen O'Connell's sway over the electorate. The tithe was a great century-old injustice; that a Catholic peasant should have to pay it to an Anglican minister was bad enough, but the constant presence of the assessors, or proctors, and their rapacity, rubbed salt into the wound. When Scotland also had to agree to the Union in 1707, at least it was her own national Presbyterian Church which was recognized by the State. Against this abuse of the tithe, which on more than one occasion led to brawls and bloodshed, O'Connell could do nothing, or anyway very little; at last, in 1838, the tithe was included in the rent and passed on by the landlord, which lessened the friction but not the abuse. All this time, O'Connell, who only believed in peaceful, constitutional methods, was managing to persuade these rough, harassed, excitable peasants, whose fathers had fought in 1798, that violence would be unwise, unlawful, and useless and would only end by bringing trouble on its authors; they listened to their master, who was almost a god to them; and he, when he returned to the English House of Commons, was able to claim that under him outrages were growing rarer every day.

Nevertheless, interest was now turning towards the social question; how was this oppression system of ownership to be reformed? And, in order to reform it, was it necessary for the isalnd first of all to reestablish a government of its own? The coming to power of Lord Melbourne, a well-intentioned Whig, made O'Connell decide to give the Union one more chance, and he was confirmed in this view by the fact that there was, at the Castle, Lord Mulgrave, a viceroy of just character, who had in Drummond an excellent undersecretary; the latter treated each confession with impartiality and had dared to write to a noble landlord reminding him that "property has its duties as well as its rights." When Drummond was dead and Mulgrave had fallen, the time had come to reconsider the tactics. The association for revoking the Act of the Union, the "Repeal Association," was rapidly gaining ground in the country. On the other hand, O'Connell could see—and this was by no means pleasing to him—that the Young Ireland editors of the *Nation* were coming to the fore alongside him (1842), Gavan Duffy, Davis, Mitchel, and the poet Mangan; they followed him, certainly, but they also were watching him, a form of supervision which was to push him further and faster than he wished to go. He had, against his better judgment, to move a motion for the repeal in the House of Commons, and, as he had foretold, was severely defeated.

He then began to assemble those immense popular meetings in the open air, which he clearly expected would have an intimidating effect. They were unarmed, but the numbers would tell. It was not an army, but it was the material of one. He was returning to the game which had stood him in good stead in 1829. A quarter of a million came to Tara, the home of the ancient kings of Ireland. On the Sunday of October 8, 1843, O'Connell called a meeting of his men on the historic shore of Clontarf, where Brian Boru had in the old days won his battle; he was expecting a million of them. This time, however, Wellington held out; he prohibited the meeting and brought up artillery. O'Connell, who remained consistent in his horror of bloodshed, canceled his previous orders, though his people were already on the march; the partisans of force have often blamed him for this retreat, especially in the years following, but it is easy enough to blame after the event; it is certain that England, if she so wished, had at that time every means of applying repressive measures, measures which would be prompt and to which there could be no reply. O'Connell spared his own people a blood bath, one which would have served no purpose. After that, he was old and tired out and had outlived his legend. The immense catastrophe of the famine was beginning to show its face. He was on his way to find fresh strength at the See of the Apostle, when destiny overtook him at Genoa and he died (1847).

Chapter 18.   Parnell

The Young Ireland group, some of them Protestants, were somewhat different in their outlook from O'Connell and in certain aspects nearer to Wolfe Tone, in that they aspired above all to independence and the reconquest of the soil. From the generation of 1848 they had inherited its uncompromising and generous idealism, but its illusions as well. At the same time, they also differed from Wolfe Tone, in that they sought for their inspiration in the national history of Ireland and even in its legends; they transcribed into English, this new language of the people, the Gaelic love for *Dark Rosaleen*. They were poets, and as is the way with poets, peremptory in character. Thus came about their quarrel with the old chief, whom they regarded as vacillating and who regarded them as dangerous.

Their differences were not so much interrupted as wiped out by the immense disaster of the famine. The peasants, who had been bled dry by excessive rents and who had to export their corn in order to raise the money to pay them, lived on potatoes and were unable to put by any reserves. The country was seriously overpopulated, and the population badly distributed, being specially congested in the most barren regions, on the Atlantic coast. If the potato crop were to fail, there would immediately be a famine. Now, during three successive years, 1845, 1846, and 1847, a blight began to appear in the plants. Relief measures came too late and were too slight; this may have been because of the English being unaware of how great the peril was, or because of a state of mental stagnation caused by the economic axioms of the age, which could not conceive of any form of state action interfering with the free play of economic forces. The people died by tens of thousands, some of them from actual starvation but more from diseases due to malnutrition, fevers, dysentery, and cholera. Others, in order to save their lives, emigrated in large numbers, 100,000 in 1846, 200,000 per year from 1847 to 1850, 250,000 in the single year of 1851; those who had already emigrated saved the price of the passage for their relatives who had stayed behind, and the hemorrhage set in which would stop no more. In three years the population fell to six and a half millions. And then, by an incredible aberration, the corn which could have saved so many lives went over from Ireland to England, in order to provide the rent for the landlord. It must be said in their honor that a number of landowners did their duty and remained among their people, mortgaging everything in their efforts to assist them. In 1849 Parliament had to pass a special act in order to deal with the ruin of their estates. Most of these passed into the hands of new landowners, often enough businessmen who saw in them no more than investment and took no interest in the people or their customs. With these new landlords, evictions became more frequent than ever; there was a Mr. Adair who at Glenveigh in 1861 drove out 700 people at the point of the bayonet. It is not surprising that in 1881 the census figures showed a drop to five millions, and since then they have, by a slow but steady decline, almost dropped to four—the figures of 1800, or perhaps rather less. The habit of going away was formed.

There was another aspect to the famine; it gave the last blow to the Gaelic language. In the middle of the century it was widely spoken west of a line running from Cork to Derry; but those who spoke it were precisely those who died or emigrated, the peasants. The primary schools taught them only English by law. The Established Church had attempted a proselytizing movement through the language, so that the priests advised their people to cease speaking that which might endanger their souls. And O'Connell, as we have seen, only saw in it an obstacle to progress. O'Connell, the schools, the Church, the famine, emigration—they were too much for it, and the Gaelic language began its long death struggle. It was reckoned that in 1850 a million and a half were still faithful to it; round about 1900, 600,000; today, how many?

However, the revolution of 1848 was shaking the thrones all over Europe. The Young Ireland party thought that the time for secession had come. William Smith O'Brien who, though a member of Parliament, a landlord, and a Protestant, was descended from the former Gaelic kings of Thomond, had been outraged by the famine scenes which he had witnessed in County Clare; he went off to Paris and artlessly asked Lamartine for his alliance. Having met with a polite refusal, he tried to raise a rebellion in Munster. It was a wild venture: a few were killed, others were tried, Smith O'Brien, Mitchel, and Gavan Duffy were condemned to death, reprieved, and deported. Young Ireland was no more.

An uneasy period followed, under a surface of gloom. A system of public education was slowly being evolved. The Act of 1850 widened the franchise to include new categories of electors. In the same year a league was founded to defend the rights of the farmers, the aim of which was to obtain the three F's, Fair Rent, Fixity of Tenure, and Free Sale, which in fact meant that the old customs of Ulster should be extended to the whole country; the small farmer would have a guarantee that, as long as he paid his rent he could not be put out, he would have a right in regard to the improvements for which he had been responsible, and a right to buy his farm if it were to be sold. When he became Prime Minister in 1869, Gladstone took a step in this direction— but no more than a step. Besides, Gladstone, who was a convinced Anglican, certainly behaved in the most just fashion when he withdrew from his own Church the official monopoly in Ireland; she was to be left with endowments amounting to about £10,000,000, but she ceased to be the official Church, and thus lost the right of levying tithes on those whom she could not claim as her members.

But the age of concessions, compromises, and half measures had run its course. The new generation was not calling for better landlords but that there should be no landlords at all, and the land given to the peasants; not for a better government, but for a government of their own, for independence, for "the Republic"—such was the meaning of the words. And the agrarian troubles went on. Besides, the American Civil War had a considerable influence in Ireland. A number of emigrants from the famine had taken part in it, some of them in the first rank; they had no love for England and, not content with having brought the case of Ireland to where it now was, before the world, they had sworn to come back and fight for her on their native soil. Their ideal, which from then onwards was republican, went back to Wolfe Tone or, more briefly, was the same as America's. In Ireland it inspired John O'Leary, O'Dovovan Rossa, and Kickham, the leaders of the Fenians who were named after the Fianna, legendary defenders of epic Ireland. A secret society, the Irish Republican Brotherhood, was making plans for a rising. This broke out in March

1867 but was a feeble affair which soon proved abortive; England herself received a few hits. There were no executions, only long sentences of imprisonment. Cardinal Cullen, the Archbishop of Dublin, a prelate who had received his formation in Rome and was Ultramontane in spirit, had, with the hierarchy behind him, condemned the movement, even to the point of excommunication. Nevertheless, in 1861, when the body of Terence MacManus was brought back from St. Patrick's, New York, a vast crowd followed the procession to Glasnevin and thus showed where the heart of Ireland lay; indeed, after their defeat, perhaps because of it, the Irish people looked on the Fenians with gratitude and tenderness and held them in honor with constant fidelity.

About that time one Isaac Butt, a Protestant lawyer who had fought his first battles under O'Connell, founded a party of compromise based on the idea of Home Rule; instead of complete independence, which for the moment was out of the question, would not local autonomy, with Ireland still remaining within the United Kingdom, be a solution acceptable to everyone? Ireland would be doubly represented, at Westminster for imperial affairs, in Dublin for her own; the Union would thus be replaced by a federal bond. The picturesque figure of the party was one Joseph Biggar, who was prepared to talk interminably about anything or nothing, with the sole aim of blocking the Parliamentary debates. In 1875 a new recruit appeared on the scene, Charles Stewart Parnell, who had been returned as a member for Meath; he was still quite a young man, under 30, tall and slim, with haughty good looks—his portrait can still be seen hanging on the walls of many an Irish inn—who was able to impress his personality on others by his reserve, his disdain, and his silence, even more than O'Connell with

his eloquence and his sarcasm. Within two years he had
replaced Butt as leader, and under him the Irish party,
which up to then had been rather soft and ineffectual in
its purely constitutional activities, and had won the contempt of the Fenian remnant, took on an unaccustomed
vigor. To everyone's surprise, Parnell joined Biggar in
his strange tactics, but he immediately combined it with a
technical skill (knowledge of the rules and careful choice
of the debates to be obstructed) which rendered it far
more dangerous; for a danger it certainly was, in a
machine which was already too slow for the stuff it was
supposed to grind and the wheels of which were clogging
with sand. Then, apart from this official sabotage, there
was Parnell's inimitable manner, proud and icy, no
longer that of a subject seeking favors but that of an equal,
indignantly demanding what was due. Finally, there was
the fact that Parnell, a Protestant and a landlord, was
clearly paying no attention to his own interests or to
those of his class and, like Swift and Grattan before him,
and for the same reasons, was carrying the country away
with enthusiasm. A second "uncrowned king" had appeared, so different from the other and perhaps even
more loved and worshiped.

Under his leadership the Parliamentary battle was
fought with a pugnacity which delighted even the partisans of physical force and renewed the alliance between
them and those who believed in constitutional methods, a
gain of the first importance. Besides, behind the legal
agitation a campaign of violence was in full swing; the
evictions were countered with the "example" made of
Captain Boycott, even with the murder of specially hated
landowners, such as the inflexible Lord Leitrim, whose
assassins were never found (1878). Parnell fully understood how profoundly interdependent were the social and

the national battles, and he fought together the battle
for the land and that for freedom. His best lieutenant,
Michael Davitt, the son of an evicted peasant, who had
been a laborer in an English factory and had only recently been set free from an English prison, was the
leader of the Land League (1879). His teaching was
that property, the very soil, should be returned to the
farmer who ploughed it, to the Gael who had owned it
in the old days. Besides, Parnell had met with a conscience in London, Gladstone, a man of deep piety,
whose fundamental sense of justice was urging him on to
right the wrongs of Ireland. His law of 1881 reduced the
rents, granted the three F's, and recognized that the
tenants had rights parallel with those of the landlords.
As they now found themselves forsaken right up to the
House of Lords, the landlords came to prefer the idea of
transferring their land to the peasants, which transfer
should be guaranteed by the state. This brought about
the law of 1891 dealing with the redemption of the land.

The war for autonomy was waged simultaneously. A
majority of the Commons and almost the whole of the
Lords were against it. The assassination of Lord Fred-
erick Cavendish and Mr. Burke, the Secretary and Under
Secretary for Ireland, in May 1882 was an error which
hardened English opinion; a proof of this is that four
years laters, letters—which turned out to be forgeries—
were published by the *Times,* attempting to implicate
Parnell as being in connivance with the terrorists.
Nevertheless, in the elections of 1885 he was returned
to Westminster with 86 stalwarts. Gladstone took the
plunge and in 1886 presented the Commons with a
scheme for Home Rule, but was defeated and fell. The
Conservatives came to power, with Arthur Balfour as
Chief Secretary, and were determined to maintain the

Union; they relied on repressive methods for dealing with the extremists and on benevolence and friendly attentions for the others.

Suddenly, Parnell stumbled: a legal action revealed his liaison with Mrs. O'Shea and caused a scandal. Gladstone refused to cooperate with him any further; should his reaction not seem to be altogether coherent, in that it was public, while concerned with a strictly private matter, it should not be forgotten that were it not for his all pervading moral sense there would not have been the Gladstone whose chief care, in regard to Ireland, was to make justice prevail. The Catholic Church could not remain behind, and the bishops condemned Parnell. A division immediately appeared among his own people as deep, as violent, and as envenomed as that which was caused later by the Dreyfus affair in France; hatreds broke out between brothers which 30 years later were still unquenched. Parnell, with his inflexible tenacity, was fighting the whole time to recover his position. Death interrupted him; he was 45 years old.

Chapter 19. *Sinn Fein*

In the following year (1892) Gladstone, who remained obstinately true to his principles, presented a new Home Rule Bill to the Commons, and it was passed. In the Lords there was a crushing adverse vote. Gladstone, having fallen, died; for the next ten years and even longer the idea, which had been found unfeasible, disappeared from the field of practical politics. The times were dreary. The Irish Party was tearing itself out with internal divisions; Redmond, backed by a small minority,

Sinn Fein   123

fought on the side of Parnell, and Dillon against. As
for the country, its condition was being gradually im-
proved by reforms. Agriculture was prospering under the
influence of the cooperative movement led by Sir
Horace Plunkett and George Russell (AE). The generous
Wyndham Act of 1903, which offered state subsidies
repayable in 68 annuities, themselves lower than the
legal rents, completed the dividing up of the great estates
among the farmers, who now became the possessing
class, while the establishment of the County Councils
in 1898 had already transferred the administration into
their hands from those of the landlords. The system of
public education was being completed at every level.
This dated from a long while back. Primary education
had been organized for the first time in 1831, the school
in each parish being placed directly under the care of the
religious authority, whether the parson or the parish
priest; the intention was good, in that it aimed at avoiding quarrels, but unfortunate, in that it perpetuated the
split which was already in existence. In 1845, in order to
meet the demand for a higher education apart from that
of Trinity College, which was held to be Protestant, Sir
Robert Peel opened the three queen's Colleges at Galway,
Cork, and Belfast, all three of which were to be nonconfessional, in order to avoid friction; the bishops
placed them under a ban, precisely for this reason, and
in 1854, with the assistance of Newman, they themselves
founded the Catholic University, which did not prosper;
at last, in 1908, the National University was founded, with
its three colleges of Galway, Cork, and Dublin,[15] which,

[15] Belfast became independent, under the name of Queen's University, and Maynooth, being an establishment with university
status, was joined to the National University as an approved college.

though still nonconfessional according to its charter, had
an atmosphere that satisfied the Catholics and they
flocked to it immediately. Secondary education had, as
in England, continued to be a private enterprise and was
mainly in the hands of the religious orders; the Intermediate Education Office was established in 1878, in
order to try and keep it at a fairly unifrom level, and was
entrusted with the task of holding common examinations,
according to results of which, subsidies were paid to the
schools. Owing to the constant fear of misunderstandings,
the members of the Office were exactly half Catholic and
half Protestant, and controversial subjects were pro-
scribed, in particular the history of Ireland, especially of
modern times. Was this also the reason why philosophy
was not included? One can well imagine that as the result of such a policy, education tended to be rather
anemic; the system also had a defect of a peculiarly
British type, which was that, apart from the primary
schools, education had to be paid for and was expensive.
But when viewed as a whole, what a contrast with the
illiteracy which in the previous century had been deliberately enforced on the Gaelic masses.

If Ireland, pregnant with the future, was in spite of
this treatment secretly on the move, it was no longer in
the same direction as the Irish party, which was imbued,
especially under Redmond, with the spirit of conciliation
and compromise. On the one hand, there was a revival
of the love which the Young Ireland group, Davis and
the others, had had for the most ancient Gaelic past; this
was assisted by the work of learned men which was
bringing to light the ancient texts, now translated and
given to the public; such were, for example, the great
and talented Standish Hayes O'Grady and the poetical
school which acknowledged Yeats as its master and in-

cluded such varied types as AE, Lady Gregory, Synge,
and even in a much more restricted sense, George Moore.
This revival of interest in its traditions secured for the
country the foundation of the Gaelic League by Douglas
Hyde (1893), the program of which was to save the
ancient language from the perils threatening it, either
by preserving it among the 500,000 souls who still spoke
it, or by teaching it once more to the Anglicized masses.
As can be imagined, this *félibrige*[16] (for such it certainly
was) was soon won over by those engaged in active
politics, who realized that a separate language is the
surest evidence of nationality and also its guarantee. On
the other hand, an original form of political thought
was beginning to appear from the pen of Arthur Griffith
in his *United Irishman* (1899). The man had reflected
on the spot (in South Africa) on the relations between a
Dominion and the Metropolis within the Empire, while
he had studied in books how Hungary, under the leadership of Francis Deak, had broken loose from Austria. At
that time he would have been content with a wide meas-
ure of autonomy, the kingdom of Ireland being linked to
the other in a personal union, under the King as head.
The methods that he recommended for attaining this may
at first seem strange: the national representatives should
abstain from appearing at Westminster and sit at home,
while in Ireland, far from embarking on an armed rising, which could have no hope of success, the people
should limit themselves obstinately to passive resistance,
such as the boycotting of English goods. To this doctrine
he himself gave the name of *Sinn Fein,* which means
"Ourselves" or "We Alone" (1906).

However, at this juncture things had a more favorable

16 This word has no English equivalent. It refers to the revival of
Provençal literature [Translator].

look in London. The Lords had thrown out the "people's
budget" which had been drawn up by Lloyd George, so
Asquith, in order to overcome them, wished to leave
them from henceforward with only a temporary veto.
Now, two general elections, in January and December
1910, left him at the mercy of the Labor and Irish
members. The reform was passed, even by the Lords,
under threat of being swamped by new peers (1911).
The Lords, who up till then had blocked every scheme
for Home Rule, were left with a merely suspensory power,
while on the other hand Asquith depended on the Irish
vote. He put forward a fresh scheme for Home Rule,
which was passed by the same coalition in the Commons
and thrown out by the Lords; but if passed on two
further occasions by the Commons, in 1914 it would
have the force of law. At that moment, Ulster, quite
deliberately, threw down the gauntlet.

How that Ulster had changed, since the old days when
it had been the first to rise in answer to Wolfe Tone's
appeal! Its Presbyterian element, who had been the real
Liberals of that day, had, in their disappointment, started
to reflect, and whether rightly or wrongly, imagined that
they could discern a confessional and thus an anti-
Protestant note in the 1798 rebellion. The endemic
brawls between the "Peep of Day Boys" and the "Defenders" had embittered matters yet further. The grant,
under Castlereagh, of a *Regium Donum* large enough to
provide their ministers with suitable stipends had brought
them closer to their brethren, the Anglicans, who had
formerly been their enemies. One of their pastors, Cooke,
whose gifts as an orator and a popular leader were
scarcely inferior to O'Connell's, had confirmed them in
this new tendency, with such success that Daniel O'Connell hardly dared to appear in their country. The Orange

movement had won them over. Fearing, and it was not improbable, that Home Rule, with its Papist majority, would be the end of Protestant rule—which they held that they could anyway maintain in their little corner, where they predominated—they refused to submit to the decision of Parliament. Protestant Ulster was, in fact, in a state of revolt. It owed its inspiration to Sir Edward Carson, a successful barrister who had moved up from Dublin to the North and who provided them with the motto of "Not an inch." In 1913 his irregulars occupied Larne and Donaghadee in order to unload a cargo of arms. Redmond, disturbed by this fresh threat, was also raising his volunteers; when the latter in their turn came back from Howth with the rifles which they had smuggled in, they were met by the British troops, who fired on them. Everything was pointing to civil war. All the more so, in that when the garrison at the Curragh received orders to move up to Ulster, 50 officers, with General Gough at their head, preferred to resign their commissions rather than obey. And then the war, the great one, the real one, broke out.

Redmond immediately pledged the support of his followers: let his volunteers be armed and officered, and they would defend the country. Kitchener, who was suspicious, did nothing of the kind. And then, as things turned out, the volunteers were not all of the same mind. The majority followed Redmond, on whose word they relied, and served with distinction on the battlefields of Flanders. A smaller but determined number refused to "fight under an alien flag" and, recalling Spain in the sixteenth century and France in the eighteenth, declared that they had no quarrel with Germany, who might indeed prove useful. . . . To these latter the Home Rule Bill seemed to be merely the same old played-

out farce: it now reserved the right of secession for six
Ulster counties, on which condition alone it had received the royal assent, and having in due form become
law, it would not be put into effect till after the end of
hostilities. Another sign of the times was that in 1915
Sir Edward Carson entered the War Cabinet.

There was a new thought coming to birth among a
small nucleus of the volunteers, a thought belonging to
idealists and poets and not to calculating men, which, as
things turned out, was to have a wider reach and to look
further than any calculation. Their leader was Patrick
Pearse, a man of humble and *English* origin (like so
many Irish leaders!) but son of an Irish mother; he was
familiar with Connemara and, over there, in that ancient,
immemorial country, had drunk the philter of the
language and the tradition. He was a Gaelic poet, the
founder of a school where all the teaching was given in
Gaelic, and he was convinced that this placid, drowsy
Ireland, to whom they were always advertising the material advantages of Home Rule, must be awakened from
her rumination and her soul restored to her. This could
be done in one way alone, the offering of blood: a small
band of enthusiasts, or confessors, shall we say, would
prove to the world, would prove to Ireland herself, that
she was worth dying for. In 1803 Robert Emmet had
succeeded in nothing—except in his death, but that had
been enough to rouse in the country that long shudder
by which she was still stirred. This was a mystical conception, which to some may appear flaming and romantic
but can be explained by Gaelic history and poetry and
also the Gaelic mentality; Pearse and his companions
Plunkett and MacDonagh were poets, while Connolly, in
his Marxism, was a theorist rather than a politician:
Ireland might perhaps give but one cry, yet that cry

would, without tricks or shams, claim the whole of her rights.

The rising was planned for Easter Monday, 1916. Sir Roger Casement, who had gone to Berlin to seek for aid, understood that on the contrary Germany would make use of Ireland without seriously trying to do anything for her, and returned in a submarine, having definitely decided to call off the adventure; he was captured on landing and later was executed. The insurgents failed to capture the Castle but seized the Post Office, where they proclaimed the Republic and, after a week of fighting, surrendered. There were 500 dead, and the center of Dublin had been burnt down. Sir John Maxwell, who was Commander-in-Chief, caused sixteen of the insurgents to be court-martialed and shot. But Pearse dead was more dangerous than Pearse alive: with his deep understanding of the people he had foreseen that the revulsion would bring Ireland round.

This was to be clearly seen in February 1917, when at a bye-election Redmond's candidate was not elected, but defeated by Count Plunkett, the father of one of the sixteen. In Clare a little later de Valera, who had been condemned to death, then reprieved, and was serving his jail sentence in England, replaced Redmond's own brother, who had been killed on the Flanders front. The war dragged on, the viceroy, Lord French, threatened to apply conscription, which was now imposed by law in the United Kingdom; the whole country rose in indignation at this (how its temper had changed within the last three years!) and the law yielded: a lesson which was not forgotten. . . . At the elections following the armistice, the new movement, which was the heir of Easter 1916, swept everything before it. Redmond had died; out of 105 members of Parliament only eight of his own followers

still held their seats, while 73, who had adopted Pearse's
doctrines and Griffith's tactics, swore that they would not
take their seats at Westminster; they sat in Dail Eireann,
or Assembly of Ireland, and once again proclaimed the
Republic or Ireland, with de Valera, who for the time
being was in prison at Lincoln, as its President. London
pretended not to take the matter seriously; Wilson had
recently shown out the Irish delegation who were claiming a right to sit at the Peace Conference; there was thus
the curious phenomenon in Ireland of an official government which was losing its grip of the country, while
there was another, an underground government, which,
whether through persuasion or fear, was gaining in authority every day.

Something had to be done. Lloyd George caused an
amendment to be passed to the Home Rule Bill, by which
Southern Ireland should govern herself, with Carson's
Ulster excluded. This amendment became law in the au-
tumn of 1920 and divided the island into two states of
unequal size: the South consisted of 26 counties and
was to have its own legislative assembly, while the North,
which consisted of only six counties, was to have two
kinds of representation; local affairs would be dealt with
at Stormont, and the Union preserved at Westminster. The
arrangement has lasted to this day, and from it is derived
the new title of "King of the United Kingdom of Great
Britain and Northern Ireland." But scarcely anybody
came to the Assembly of "Southern Ireland" which the
viceroy convoked in Dublin.

And then the revolver shots rapped out: the police
were fired at on the pretext that as they were recruited
in Ireland they were traitors. The police replied, and
guerilla warfare gradually became an established thing.
London was very ill at ease: should they go to war? But

against whom and in the name of what, since the resur-
rection of the ancient nations was being promoted everywhere in Europe? And then it was necessary to mind
American opinion, which was always inclined to be suspicious and very sensitive to Irish pressure. Finally, the best
British opinion—that of the Liberals and of the Church
—was not very proud of the spectacle which Ireland presented. Having shrunk from real war, the British resigned
themselves to counterguerilla warfare, which proved to be
no small blunder. Two special bodies were recruited,
one of police, which was nicknamed the Black and Tans,
in memory, it was said, of a famous pack of hounds, and
the other of ex-officers, which was known as the Auxil-
iaries; and then there began, on each side, a campaign of
ambushes and executions, of reprisals and replies, so that
it seemed impossible to conceive how there could be any
end to this monotonous small-scale hell. This time, however, it proved too much for English public opinion; an
English general even resigned his command; in July 1921
a truce was concluded and negotiations were opened,
with Lloyd George on one side and de Valera on the
other, and later Michael Collins and Griffith. They ended,
after months of difficult discussions and threatened break-
downs, with the treaty of December 6; the Saorstat
Eireann, the Free State of Ireland, was given the full
status of a Dominion within the Empire, with complete
control of its finances and fighting forces, a condition
based exactly on that enjoyed by Canada. The British
navy reserved only for itself the use of four fortified ports
and their adjacent airfields. Northern Ireland, as defined
by the law of 1920, retained her right of secession,
which she exercised. But at last the Irish had *a treaty,* a
thing which was of capital importance, because this fact
alone recognized in Ireland a contracting party with

whom it could be signed and thus recognized her as a state.

When they returned, however, de Valera repudiated his representatives, because they had accepted allegiance to the Crown and inclusion within the Empire. Dail Eireann, when it assembled, voted against him by a small margin, 64 votes to 57. Griffith became President in his place, with Collins as his right-hand man, and after a period of long and confused disputes, civil war broke out. Griffith died in August 1922, Collins was killed a few days later, and Cosgrave succeeded them; at the end of a year, which had been fairly prolific in bloody encounters, the insurrection died out, having come to the end of its resources. Cosgrave ruled; he frankly accepted Dominion status, and the frontier between Ireland and her recalcitrant remnant was traced out in detail under him. De Valera and his followers, who were being elected in slowly increasing numbers, boycotted the Dail, which they held to be illegal, and refused to take the oath of allegiance to the King. In 1927, under threat of having their elections annulled if they persisted in not fulfilling their mandates, they resigned themselves to entering the Irish Parliament.

In 1932, having obtained a relative majority, which later became absolute, they assumed power, first in a coalition with Labor and then on their own. They kept it till the end of 1947. De Valera had obtained a hold on the imaginations and affections of the people scarcely less than that of O'Connell or Parnell. His policy has been to affirm ever more strongly, using every possible expedient, the sovereign status of Ireland; for instance, he replaced Cosgrave's governor-general, who had himself replaced the viceroy, by an elected president, and changed the title of Free State to that of Eire. This independent attitude gained strength during the last war, through the neutrality which he obstinately observed, in spite of every pressure, even that from America. In his home policy, de Valera, the heir of Young Ireland and the Gaelic League, did all that a government could do to restore to the ancient language the vitality which it was losing; in vain, so it would seem—its spiritual values are unable to outweigh the practical and technical values of English. The State of Ireland, like all others, has been slowly socialized; de Valera increased the expense of government year by year, to a point at which one is inclined to think that the excessive weight of taxation brought about his fall. It is Cosgrave's old partisans, succeeding de Valera, owing to a strange but necessary alliance with the Left, who, with no very lively reaction on the part of the London Labour Cabinet, have definitely ruled the King of England out of Irish affairs and have, without any reserve whatsoever, declared the Republic of Ireland—thus, in a sense, returning, after almost eight centuries, to the independence of the days before the Plantagenets.

Epilogue

Nobody is more conscious than the author of what is lacking in this study; it has been deliberately restricted, as far as was possible, to depicting successive stages of civilization, leaving out the infinite detail of the facts, which it would have been futile to try and include in the small space at our disposal; the emphasis has been laid, maybe mistakenly, on things Gaelic, because it was in them, in those ways of life, of thought and of art that Ireland was a unique figure, without match or equal in the modern age, and because their loss is something that will never be retrieved . . . When that died, Ireland became but another bit of Europe.

This history of Ireland is a sad tale, as if she were the victim of an evil spell, moving through the centuries from misfortune to misfortune, unable, it would seem, to achieve equilibrium, to reach a solution. "The sea keeps

135

us from unity," said Grattan, thinking of the English,
"but the ocean imposes it on us." [17] If this is more than a
mere turn of phrase, if it really is Ireland's destiny to be
one of the "British Isles," what is it that in her case has
prevented a friendly agreement with England, like that
between England and Scotland, who for so long were at
daggers drawn? Is there some curse on her? For, after
all, usurpations, acts of violence, and massacres are, alas!
the common thread running through all past histories.
How is it that in her case the wounds have not healed? It
is certainly not because she was more brutally treated, for
what can surpass the harshness of the days after Culloden
and the deeds of "Butcher Cumberland"? It is, I think,
that England was guilty of a double error: in Scotland the
conquered were not robbed of their land, and attempts
to meddle with their faith soon came to an end. When
men are treated otherwise, the only way of reaching a
stable solution is to exterminate them; it is idle to imagine
that they will forever accept unbearable conditions. Now,
the "former inhabitants of the island," as Fitzgibbon
nicely called them, were not exterminated by England;
on the contrary, and here was a fresh aggravation, instead of conquering in one violent but rapid convulsion,
she went on with the slow, painful business, which with
all its clumsy details continued for centuries and was
never completed. Yet this old Ireland had, in the course
of the ages, shown an astonishing power of absorbing the
successive waves of invaders, the Vikings, the Normans,
the Mediaeval English, the Elizabethans, even the
Cromwellians; and once again we find a foreign body

---

[17] Compare this with Chateaubriand, *Mémoires d'Outre-Tombe:*
"Irlande est une chaloupe attachée au vaisseau de l'Angleterre"—
(Ireland is a launch attached to the ship of England). Is it merely
another phrase?

setting up an irritation, this obstinate Ulster, so prickly and so irreconcilable. . . .

One has the impression, as one glances backwards, that if, in spite of everything, Ireland is bound to her larger neighbor, her long and tragic history is the tragedy of lost opportunities. It is not so much that she rejected the King (on more than one occasion she fought for him); it is rather that she expected some regard, attention and love, she wished for him to be also *her* king. Over and over again it seemed that a tolerable *modus vivendi* was about to be achieved, under the Earl of Kildare, under Charles II, at the time of Grattan, or even of O'Connell; and each time, owing to some blunder, the chance was missed. Then, all attempts at mutual accommodation having failed, accounts had to be squared; on the national side, independence must be claimed; on the social side, the land must be restored to those who had formerly cared for it. These wrongs have now been righted. But there still remain over from the bloodstained past a distrust and a rancor which are slow to die out; and England has to pay a heavy price for her mistakes, for the *diaspora* of the Gaels has planted colonies throughout the world, in America, Australia, and the Argentine, which have been breeding grounds of suspicion. At the same time, owing to the dissidence of Ulster, Ireland feels that her natural unity is broken and, whether rightly or wrongly, ascribes the blame to London. What a lot of bitterness for there to be between the two countries!

And yet, if left on her own, Ireland (think merely of her exports) can scarcely hope to survive in this iron age, when only the giants grow and weakness means death. Will she continue in some way or other as a voluntary associate of the Commonwealth? Or will she join herself, a new star, to the "star-spangled banner" under which live so many of her sons, to which she is drawn by so many memories, and thus become its advance guard in the old world? Or will she try and take, like Switzerland and Sweden, the risks of a precarious isolation? Various roads are open to her. . . .

Bibliography

Alison, Phillips, W., *Revolution in Ireland*, London, 1923.

Allen, Romilly, *Celtic art and Christian times*, Archaelogia cambrensis, 1896.

Bagwell, *Ireland under the Tudors*, 3 vols., London and New York, 1890.

Bagwell, *Ireland under the Stuarts*, 3 vols., London and New York, 1916.

Barry, Tom, *Guerilla Days in Ireland*, New York, 1956.

Beaumont, G. de, *L'Irlande politique, sociale et religieuse*, Paris, 1840.

Berardis, V., *Italy and Ireland in the Middle Ages*.

Bergin, Osborn, "Bardic Poetry," *Ivernian Journal*, vol. V, no. 19.

Best, R. I., *Bibliography of Irish Philology and Literature*, Dublin, 1942.

Bieler, L., *Life and Legends of St. Patrick*.

Boyd, E. A., *Ireland's Literary Renaissance*, Dublin, 1916.

Briollay, *L'Irlande insurgée*, Paris, 1921.

Bryan, D., *The Great Earl of Kildare*, Dublin, 1933.

Bury, J. B., *Life of Saint Patrick*, London, 1905.

Butler, W., *Confiscation in Irish History*, Dublin, 1918.

139

Caldwell, J. M., *Old Irish Life,* London, 1912.

Carew, *Pacata Hibernia,* 2 vols., London, 1896.

Carleton, W., *Traits and Stories of Irish Peasantry,* London, 1896.

Chauviré, R., *L'Irlande,* Paris, 1925.

Chauviré, R., *La Geste de la Branche-Rouge,* Paris, 1926.

Chauviré, R., *Les Contes ossianiques,* Paris, 1948.

Clery, etc., *Annals of the Four Masters,* O'Donovan ed., Dublin, 1851.

Corkery, D., *The Hidden Ireland,* Dublin, 1941.

Curtis, E., *A History of Mediaeval Ireland from 1110 to 1513,* London, 1923.

Curtis, E., *A History of Ireland,* London, 1936.

Davitt, M., *Fall of Feudalism in Ireland,* London, 1904.

Demangeon, *Les Îles britanniques,* Paris, 1927.

Dinneen, *Poems of Egan O'Rahilly,* Irish Texts Society, London, 1900.

Dinneen, *Amhrain Eoghain Ruaid Ui Shuilleabhain,* Dublin, 1901.

Dottin, "La Littérature gaélique de l'Irlande," *Revue de Synthese historique,* III, VI, et VIII, 1901, 1903, et 1904.

Dottin, *Manuel de l'Antiquité celtique,* Paris, 1915.

Dottin, *Les Littératures celtiques,* Paris, 1924.

Dudley, Edwards, R., *Church and State in Tudor Ireland,* London, 1935.

Dunlop, *Ireland under the Commonwealth,* Manchester, 1913.

Edgeworth, M., *Castle Rack-rent,* Dublin, 1800.

Edgeworth, M., *Belinda,* London, 1896.

Fitzgerald, Brian, *The Geraldines,* London and New York, 1952.

Flower, R., *The Irish Tradition,* Oxford, 1947.

Froude, *The English in Ireland,* London, 1881.

Froude, *The Two Chiefs at Dunboy,* London, 1889.

Giraldus Cambrensis, *Expugnatio hibernica.*

Giraldus Cambrensis, *Topographia hibernica. Opera,* Dimock ed., 1861-1891. Dundalk, 1953.

Goblet, Y. M., *L'Irlande dans la crise universelle,* Paris, 1918.

Goblet, Y. M., *La Transformation de la géographie politique de l'Irlande au XVIIIe siècle,* Paris, 1930.

Goldsmith, *The Vicar of Wakefield,* Dublin, 1766.

Gougaud, L., *Les Chrétientés celtiques,* Paris, 1911.

Green, A. S., *Irish Nationality,* London, 1911.

Green, A. S., *Irish National Tradition,* London, 1917.

Green, A. S., *The Making of Ireland and Its Undoing,* London, 1924.

Green, A. S., *History of the Irish State to 1014,* London, 1925.

Gwynn, D., *The Irish Free State,* London, 1928.

Gwynn, S., *Highways and Byways in Donegal and Antrim,* London, 1903.

Gwynn, S., *The Fair Hills of Ireland,* London, 1906.

Gwynn, S., *The Famous Cities of Ireland,* Dublin, 1915.

Gwynn, S., *A History of Ireland,* London, 1923.

Haslip, J., *Life of Parnell,* London, 1936.

Hayden and Moonan, *A Short History of the Irish People,* Dublin, 1921.

Henry, Fr., *La Sculpture irlandaise pendant les douze premiers siècles de l'ère chrétienne,* 2 vols., Paris, 1933.

Henry, Fr., *Irish Art in the Early Christian Period,* London, 1940.

Henry, Fr., "Deux objets de bronze irlandais," *Préhistoire,* VI, pp. 65-91.

Henry, R. M., *Evolution of Sinn Fein,* Dublin, 1920.

Hoagland, Kathleen (ed)., *1000 Years of Irish Poetry,* New York, 1947.

Hubert, H., *Les Celtes et l'expansion celtique jusqu'à l'époque de La Tène,* Paris, 1932.

Hubert, H., *Les Celtes depuis l'époque de La Tene et la civilisation celtique,* Paris, 1932.

Hull, E., *A Text-book of Irish Literature,* Dublin, 1906.
Hull, E., *A History of Ireland to 1603,* 2 vols., London, 1926-1931.
Hyde, D., *A Literary History of Ireland,* London, 1899.
Hyde, D., *Irish Poetry,* Dublin, 1902.
Joyce, P. W., *Short History of Ireland,* London, 1893.
Joyce, P. W., *Social History of Ancient Ireland,* 2 vols., London, 1903.
Keating, G., *History of Ireland,* O'Connor translation, Dublin, 1841.
Kenney, J. F., *Sources for Early History of Ireland,* New York, 1929.
Kickham, *Sally Kavanagh, or the Untenanted Graves,* Dublin, 1869.
Kickham, *Knocknagow, or the Homes of Tipperary,* Dublin, 1879.
La Tochaye, *A Frenchman's Walk Through Ireland.* London, 1797.
Lecky, *History of Ireland in the XVIIIth Century,* 5 vols., London, 1897.
Le Fanu, *Seventy Years of Irish Life,* London, 1893.
Lever, Ch., *The Knight Gwynne,* London, 1864.
Lever, Ch., *Lord Kilgobbin,* 3 vols., London, 1872.
Longfield, A. K., *Anglo-Irish Trade in the XVIth Century,* London, 1929.
Lynch, J., *Cambrensis eversus,* Dublin, 1848-1852.
Mac Alister, *Ireland in the Pre-Celtic Times,* Dublin-London, 1921.
Mac Alister, *The Archeology of Ireland,* London, 1928.
Mac Alister, *Tara, a pagan sanctuary,* London, 1931.
Mac Alister, *Monasterboice,* Dundalk, 1946.
Mac Coy, H., *Scots Mercenary Forces in Ireland,* Dublin-London, 1937.
Mac Geoghegan, *Histoire de l'Irlande ancienne et moderne,* Amsterdam, 1763.
McHugh, R., *Carlow, in '98.* Dublin, 1950.

MacManus, Seumas, *The Story of the Irish Race.* Rev. ed., New York, 1944.

Mac Neill, E., "The Irish Synthetic Historians," *New Ireland,* 1906.

Mac Neill, E., *Duanaire Finn,* Part I, Irish Texts Society, London, 1908.

Mac Neill, E., *Phases of Irish History,* Dublin, 1920.

Mac Neill, E., *Celtic Ireland,* Dublin, 1921.

Mac Neill, E., *Early Irish Laws.*

Mahaffy, *An Epoch in Irish History,* London, 1903.

Maxwell, C., *A Short Bibliography of Irish History,* London, 1921.

Maxwell, C., *Irish History from Contemporary Sources, 1509-1603,* London, 1923.

Mercier, Vivian, and Greene, David H. (eds.), *1000 Years of Irish Prose,* New York, 1952.

Meyer, K., *Selections from Ancient Irish Poetry,* London.

Meyer, K., *Fianagecht,* Dublin, 1910.

Murphy, G., *Duanaire Finn,* Part II, I. T. S., London, 1933.

Murray, R. H., *Revolutionary Ireland and Its Settlement,* London, 1911.

O'Brien, B., *Life of Parnell,* London, 1898.

O'Brien, G., *The Economic History of Ireland,* 3 vols., Dublin, 1918-1921.

O'Connell, M., *The Last Colonel of the Irish Brigade,* 2 vols., London, 1892.

O'Connor, J., *Ireland,* 1798-1924, 2 vols., London, 1925.

O'Curry, E., *Lectures on the Manuscript Materials of Irish Ancient History,* Dublin, 1861.

O'Curry, E., *On the Manners and Customs of the Ancient Irish,* 3 vols., London, 1873.

O'Donovan, etc., *Ancient Laws of Ireland,* 6 vols., Dublin, 1865-1901.

O'Faolain, S., *King of the Beggars, a Life of Daniel O'Connell,* London, 1938.

O'Faolain, S., *The Great O'Neill,* London, 1942. New York.

O'Faolain, S., *The Irish, A Character Study,* New York, 1949.

O'Foghludha, R., *Brian Merriman's Cuirt and Mheadon Oidhche,* Dublin, 1912.

O'Grady, S. H., *Silva gadelica,* 2 vols., London, 1892.

O'Hegarty, P. S., *The victory of Sinn Fein,* Dublin, 1924.

O'Rahilly, T., *The Two Patricks,* Dublin, 1942.

O'Rahilly, T., *Danta Gradha,* Introduction by Robin Flower, Dublin, 1916.

O'Rahilly, T., *Early Irish History and Mythology,* Dublin, 1946.

Orpen, G., *The Song of Dermot and the Earl,* Oxford, 1892.

Orpen, G., *Ireland under the Normans,* 4 vols., Oxford, 1911-1920.

Pakenham, F., *Peace by Ordeal,* London, 1935.

Paul-Dubois, *Le Drame irlandais et l'Irlande nouvelle,* Paris, 1927.

Petrie, G., *Ecclesiastical Architecture of Ireland,* Dublin, 1845.

Prendergast, *Cromwellian Settlement,* London, 1865.

Richey, A. G., *A Short History of Ireland,* Dublin, 1887.

Ronan, M., *The Reformation in Ireland under Elizabeth,* London, 1930.

Ronan, M., *Insurgent Wicklow.*

Ryan, J., *Ireland from the Earliest Times to 800,* Dublin.

Ryan, J., *Ireland from 800 to 1600,* Dublin.

Sheehan, *The Graves at Kilmorna,* London, 1920.

Sheehan, *My New Curate,* Boston, 1925.

Sigerson, *The Last Independent Parliament of Ireland,* Dublin, 1918.

Somerville, *Some Experiences of an Irish R.M.*, London, 1901.

Somerville, *Further Experiences of an Irish R.M.*, London, 1905.

Spenser, E. D., *View of the State of Ireland, 1596*, edited by Sir James Ware, Dublin, 1633.

Stanhurst, Description of Ireland in *Holinshed's Chronicles*, 1577.

Stokes, M., *Early Christian Art in Ireland*, London, 1927.

Swift Mac Neill, *Constitutional and Parliamentary History of Ireland till the Union*, Dublin, 1917.

Thackeray, W., *The Irish Sketch-book*, 1843, London, 1879.

Thackeray, W., *The Memoirs of Barry Lindon*, London, 1879.

Thierry, Aug., *Histoire de le conquête de l'Angleterre par les Normands*, Paris, 1895.

Trench, *Realities of Irish Life*, London, 1869.

Ussher, Arland, *The Face and Mind of Ireland*, New York, 1950.

Walpole, Ch. G., *The Kingdom of Ireland*, London, 1885.

Warren, R. de, *L'Irlande et ses institutions politiques*, Paris, 1928.

Wilson, Ph., *The Beginnings of Modern Ireland*, Dublin, 1912.

Young, Arthur, *A Tour in Ireland* (1776-1779). London, 1780.